THE
GIRLS' BOOK
OF
POPULAR HOBBIES

H.R.H. Princess Alexandra—the daughter of H.R.H. The Duchess of Kent—on "Trustful" when she was 14. She is competing in the Pony Championships at the International Horse Show at the White City.

THE
GIRLS' BOOK
OF
POPULAR HOBBIES

Edited by

Ursula Bloom

BURKE ★ LONDON

ACKNOWLEDGEMENTS

The Publishers and the Editor wish to thank the following for permission to reproduce photographs:
Associated Press Ltd., Ballet Today, Baron, Camera Talks, Elsie Collins, the Editor of *Cycling*, William Davies, Keystone Press Agency Ltd., Kodak Ltd., Longmans Ltd., Mirrorpic, News Chronicle, Picture Post, Photo-Records, Press Industrial Commercial, Edward Tanner, Len Thorpe and John G. Wilson.

Burke Publishing Company Ltd.
55 Britton Street, London, E.C.1.
Printed in England by
Love & Malcomson Ltd., London and Redhill, Surrey.

CONTENTS

CONTENTS

ILLUSTRATIONS

ILLUSTRATIONS

TAKE CARE OF YOUR PET

L. Hugh Newman, F.R.E.S.

HAVING A PET OF YOUR OWN is a very great privilege, but it is also a responsibility which you must always remember. Whatever your pet may be, a dog, a cat, a rabbit, or even a tortoise, it is almost certain to give you a great deal of fun and interest, provided you do your part and look after it in the proper way.

A dog will become your friend in a way no other pet animal can ever do, but it will also need a great deal more attention. To bring up a puppy into a well-behaved dog is not at all an easy thing to do and you will need a lot of patience and must be prepared to devote much of your time to teaching your pet the various things he has to learn.

If you are given a puppy you must remember that he is only a baby and like all young creatures he needs a great deal of rest. It is both foolish and cruel to take a young puppy for long walks and it may do him much harm. Let him run about in the garden when he feels like it—that is as much exercise as he needs for the first four or five months. After this you can begin to take him for short walks on a lead to teach him how to behave in the street or on the road, but twenty minutes at a time is ample to begin with.

A dog is always very anxious to please his master or young mistress and it is a great mistake to think that you cannot train a dog without smacking him and shouting at him. Repeat the same lesson over and over again until he learns, but only for short periods, and when he gets it right make a great fuss of him and give him some little titbit as a reward. A young dog gets tired and loses interest if you worry him for hours on end, and so his lessons should not last more than a quarter of an hour or so and then he must have a good break for rest and play.

A puppy cannot grow into a strong, healthy dog unless he has the right kind of food, and so you must watch this point very carefully. While he is young he needs five or six small meals a day, but when he reaches three months you can reduce them to four, and at five months to three, and when your pet is seven months old he should be able to manage on two good meals a day. A fully-grown dog need only be fed once a day and it is generally agreed that the evening is the best time to give him his meal.

For the first three months after he has left his mother, a puppy needs plenty of milky foods, such as milk puddings left over from the family dinner or some porridge from breakfast, but it is a good plan to crumble some wholemeal bread over both dishes, so that they are not sloppy. For his midday meal you can give your puppy a little cooked, minced meat or some gravy from the dish poured over some broken-up crusts of brown bread, and if you are having fish you can offer him some of this as long as you take care to see there are no small bones in his portion!

You should never give a dog white bread, as it has been proved that this can cause fits, especially in young puppies. A large meat bone from the earliest age cannot do any harm, and your pet will enjoy gnawing at it even if he does not get much food off it and it will certainly help him with his teething troubles. From three months of age a puppy will begin to eat and enjoy liver and rabbit cut up very fine, and at four months you need no longer mince his meat but just chop it up into small pieces. Give him milk to drink at least once a day, but always have a bowl of clean water handy as well, as an over-fed puppy can get liverish and ill. Do not forget that vegetables help to keep a dog healthy, and you will soon find which kinds he will eat with his biscuits and brown bread, and which he will reject by pushing to one side of his bowl.

Do not bath your dog unless it is absolutely necessary. A dog with a short-haired coat hardly ever needs a bath, but if you own a spaniel, for example, it is sometimes a good idea to stand him in a bath of warm water and thoroughly clean the long hair on his paws and underbody without getting his back wet. But if you follow a regular routine of daily brushing and combing even this may not be necessary and your pet will be grateful, as dogs seldom like being bathed! Regular grooming, of course, keeps a dog's coat in good condition, and do not neglect the ears; the best way to clean them is to twist some cotton-wool round a matchstick and then dip it in olive oil. If your pet goes off his food and seems out of sorts, let him have plenty of water to drink and encourage him to sleep quietly. He will most likely recover in a day or two, but if he really seems ill

Regular grooming with brush and comb keeps a dog's coat in good condition.

with a dry nose and constant bouts of shivering then it is time to call in the vet.

Once your puppy has grown into a dog he will be your faithful friend for the rest of his life. Give him a warm, dry bed away from draughts, take him for a good walk every day, and never leave him for hours chained to a tree or a kennel. This is one of the things that make a dog savage. If he must be left alone during the day he should have a kennel for shelter with a good run attached, or better still leave him free to run from room to room in your house and act as a proper watch-dog. The most important thing of all to remember is never let him wander off by himself. If he gets into mischief, such as chasing sheep or even killing chickens, you, his owner, will be held responsible, and you may be fined or at the worst your dog will be ordered by the local magistrate to be destroyed and this would almost break your heart. And so make certain you always know where he is.

A young kitten is one of the most charming creatures on earth, but however playful your pet may seem, it is, like a puppy, only a baby and needs rest and quiet more than you think. Play with it by all means but not for too long and never disturb a kitten when it is lying curled up asleep. Even an old cat hates being woken up during the daytime, and although a kitten may not seem cross at the time, lack of sleep is very bad for it.

Bringing up a kitten is much easier than training a dog because it is quite useless to try to teach it any tricks—it just won't do them. The only thing you need to teach a cat is to be clean in the house, and that is usually quite easy if the training is begun early. All you need to do is to provide a shallow box filled with earth or clean ashes in the living-room, and while your pet is still quite young it will quickly learn to use it and become house-trained. As the kitten

A kitten makes a charming pet, but will seldom learn tricks like a dog.

grows older you can start putting the box outside in the garden, and most cats are intelligent enough to realize why you have done this.

A young kitten needs food every two hours and at first this should consist mainly of warm milk. Later on you can gradually introduce some cereal in the form of milk puddings, and very small quantities of minced fish and meat. As your kitten grows you will find that it does not want such frequent meals, and it is important to vary its food as much as possible, otherwise your pet is apt to become very faddy. It is a great nuisance when a cat will only eat one special kind of fish and nothing else. A full-grown cat should eat both meat scraps and fish, bread, gravy, milk puddings, rabbit, and fowl. Two meals a day are quite enough, one in the morning and another in the evening, with a bowl of milk, of course, always available.

Cats seldom follow their owners about

like dogs do, and most of them are very independent and like to do exactly as they please and come and go when they want to. They also like comfort—it is their nature. You must therefore always see that your pet has a really warm, snug bed or it will try to get into the airing cupboard or always take the best chair by the fireside and this may not be popular with other members of your family. Don't shut your cat out of doors at night! It is a great mistake to imagine that a cat always wants to wander about in the dark and cold. Sometimes it will enjoy staying out, especially on warm summer nights, but most cats prefer to be indoors in the warmth when it is cold.

Cats sometimes stray or get stolen, and it is quite a good idea to put a little collar, made from elastic, round your pet's neck with your name and address written on it in marking ink.

The ideal garden pets are undoubtedly rabbits and guinea pigs. If you live in the country or have a fairly large garden their food should cost you very little, as both these animals are strictly vegetarian. There are many different weeds you can give them to eat, such as dandelion, sowthistle, plantain, groundsel, dead nettle, chickweed, hedge parsley, and, of course, clover and grass cuttings. Rabbits are sometimes very greedy, however, especially in the early summer when the green stuff is fresh and juicy, and they may eat so much that they blow themselves out and suffer great pain and they may even die. It is up to you to see that this does not happen, by giving your hutch pets a good mixed diet, even if it costs you a little. Don't over-feed them on green-stuff, but buy some bran and oats and a regular supply of hay. In cold weather a warm mash of bran is a very good morning feed and, of course, both rabbits and guinea pigs like root vegetables. If you are giving them carrots and

turnips from the garden remember to scrub the roots clean before you feed them to your animals and be very careful not to give greens that are frosted. It is a mistake to think that rabbits do not drink water. They should always have a bowl in the hutch and this is specially important if you have a doe rabbit with babies.

It is cruel to keep a pet rabbit in a very small hutch. It should be at least three and a half feet long, eighteen inches wide and about two feet high. Very big rabbits, such as Belgian Hares or Flemish Giants, will need even more space than this. If you have a breeding doe rabbit she will need a darkened sleeping compartment at one end of the hutch as a nursery for her babies. Rabbits enjoy running about on the lawn, and in a small fenced-in garden you can very well play with your pet on the grass. But if you are away at school during the day it is best to make a wire-netting run that can be moved about on the lawn every few days. If you handle a rabbit quite a lot and always treat it gently it will become quite tame and unafraid. Never

Rabbits and guinea-pigs make ideal garden pets, as both these animals are vegetarian.

lift it up by its ears. You should always support it underneath the hind legs and lift it by the scruff of the neck.

Guinea pigs, or cavies as they are often called, can manage with smaller hutches than rabbits and as they have such short legs they don't need so much head room either. Their living quarters must be dry and draught-proof and they like a covered run, where they can play in rainy weather without getting wet. These attractive little animals like company and you can quite well keep a male and two females in the same run and there will soon be babies as well. Unlike rabbits young guinea pigs begin to run about quite soon after they are born and are very amusing little creatures to watch. Your rabbits and guinea pigs will not stay healthy unless you keep them clean. Animals like this, which are kept in hutches or rather small runs, must have their living quarters cleaned out each day so that they are kept dry and pleasant; the best covering to use on the floors of their hutches is sawdust or peat.

Tame mice are also great fun and about the only sort of pet you can carry round quite comfortably in your pocket. You can buy them both white and coloured, and if you start off with a pair you will soon be able to supply all your friends as well with mice. You can get special cages for mice, but if you have an old doll's house which you no longer play with you can convert it quite easily into a mousery. All you need to do is to put fine-mesh wire over the windows and make a trap door and ladder leading from the ground floor upstairs. Cut a piece of lino to fit the floor and cover this with sawdust and everything is ready for your pets.

Compared with rabbits and cavies, mice eat very little, and the best food to give them is a mixture of rolled oats and bird seed with a few drops of cod-liver oil added. They like to nibble on and off all

Give your rabbits a regular supply of bran, oats and hay—don't overfeed them on green-stuff.

day and night, so keep their food dish always well filled. Don't forget to give them water and they are very fond of a little cabbage stalk or a lettuce leaf now and then. It is a great mistake to give mice, cheese. They do not need it in their diet and it only makes them smell.

If you should find a hedgehog roaming around, and especially if it is a young one, you can quite well make a pet of it. These animals are nearly always badly infested with fleas so, first of all, you must give your hedgehog a good dusting with Gammexane powder, which is harmless to animals but kills insects. A summerhouse or garden shed is a good place to keep a hedgehog, but in a small enclosed garden you can allow it to roam where it likes, and it will not harm the flowers because it feeds only on insects, worms, and slugs.

Milk, or bread and milk, is a favourite dish with these prickly little animals and they also like eggs and all kinds of fish and meat scraps.

In late autumn hedgehogs like to hide away and go into hibernation, and if you provide your pet with a good heap of dry grass and leaves he will burrow down into it and make himself a warm weatherproof "sleeping-bag". Once he has retired for the winter leave him alone. He will wake up of his own accord again in the spring and then you can begin feeding him with all the things he likes best.

Tortoises, too, are summertime pets for the garden and should be encouraged to sleep the winter away packed in a big wooden box of straw or dry leaves. Unlike hedgehogs they are entirely vegetarian and so it is *not* a good plan to let them wander everywhere in the garden at will, because they will undoubtedly find the lettuces. You should try to construct some kind of a tortoise house as the illustration on this page shows and confine them to one part of the lawn with a little, low wooden fence. They will keep the weeds down on your lawn, especially the dandelions which they appear to like more than anything else. Do not forget that tortoises are fond of water for drinking and bathing, so you should provide a shallow dish so that they can climb right in and have a bath.

It is not always easy for a girl to make a kennel or a rabbit hutch or even a tortoise house, but fathers, uncles, or brothers can often be persuaded to give a hand and very probably they will do the whole job for you, if they see that you are really keen to keep a pet.

Make a house for your tortoises and confine them to one part of the lawn.

WRITING FOR YOUR HOBBY

Catherine Bell

TAKE SOMETHING TO WRITE with, something to write on, and that's all the equipment you need if writing is to be your hobby. And what a satisfactory hobby writing can be. You can "let off steam", give vent to your feelings, pour out your heart on to paper, and put all the thoughts that come tumbling into your mind into cold storage for another day.

Wouldn't it be wonderful if at the age of thirty-four or forty-four you could re-capture in an instant just what it feels like to be fourteen all over again? It would be quite easy if at fourteen writing was your hobby, if you used an exercise book for a journal, and every now and then you wrote down a graphic account of your home life, your school activities, thoughts and feel-ings.

You may not know much about life in seventeenth-century London, of how people felt during the Great Fire. But go to any Public Library and take down a copy of Samuel Pepys' Diary. Almost im-mediately you can capture the simple, everyday atmosphere of the Pepys' house-hold and of the author's home life. In his diaries will be found not only news of his-torical interest, of doings at the Admiralty, at Court, but day-to-day accounts of his own home life, domestic tiffs with his wife, the musical shortcomings of his friends, his amusements and pleasures. "Home, and being washing-day, dined upon cold meat." You may not be another Samuel Pepys, but if you have a flair for writing you can lay up a wonderful gift for your-self in later life by putting a little of your-self as you are now into cold storage, and what is a diary but a particle of yourself today put into cold storage for tomorrow?

Would you like to visit Baghdad, the South of France, or Northern Ontario? Perhaps it's unlikely that you'll get far-ther than Torquay or Blackpool for a summer holiday. If you find letter-writing no hardship, there's no reason why you shouldn't get to know something of life overseas. Why not apply to the editor of one of the girls' magazines that run Pen-pal schemes? Ask to be put in touch with a girl your own age in the country that in-trigues you most. The two of you may never meet, but by the regular exchange of letters you may become the closest of friends. You can give a faithful picture of your home life and interests here, and feel that she, in the same way, is sharing her home and family with you.

Shyness makes it difficult for many girls to make friends easily, but although they find it hard to chatter and relax with people they meet, when it comes to letter-writing they forget to be self-conscious and get endless pleasure from exchanging news and views with pen-friends. If you have no particular friends of your own age near you, you could ask to be put in touch with another girl in England, whose interests and hobbies are similar to your own.

Possibly you are nursing a secret ambi-tion to become a novelist, or a playwright, and you have the urge to keep scribbling, scribbling, scribbling. Those were the words of a Royal rebuke, "Scribbling, scribbling, always scribbling!" It was ad-

Ursula Bloom published her first book when she was only seven and decided to make writing her vocation from this early age.

dressed to Edward Gibbon, whose reply was his *Decline and Fall of the Roman Empire*. If you have the urge to write, then by all means write, but remember that writing is a craft, and all crafts have to be learned. In the words of Alexander Pope:

> True ease in writing comes from
>   art, not chance,
> As those move easiest who have
>   learned to dance.

It is true that the main requirements for a writer are merely pen and paper, but there is more to it than that. It takes more than a pen to make a writer, more than a little mind in a small room. If you want to write, you must read, get out, meet people. It takes all sorts of men and women to make one author.

There are many who say: "If only I had time, I'm sure I could write!" You may have exams. to work for, but if you have a gift for writing, use it to help you pass your exams. You may find geography tiresome, history books dull, or botany a trial. Put your writing to good account by compiling your own history book, your own geography essays. Use your school text-books as reference books to get your facts right, and in the same way as a biographer collects notes from other written works for his biography, use your school text-books as a guide, note down the essential details, and present them again in your own words. Write up your own geography essays, historical pen pictures, and nature notes. It will help impress the facts on your mind, and it's a good exercise of the hobby of your choice.

Can you sternly criticise what you have written? A self-critical faculty is a most important asset to a writer. It's so easy to find fault with others, so difficult to find fault with oneself. In one of his letters to

his mother, Matthew Arnold criticised the poet Swinburne:

> His fatal habit of using one hundred words where one would suffice always offends me.

So many aspiring writers have that failing; they get carried away with enthusiasm and use so many words that the reader is quite swamped. It is the quality of writing, not quantity, that makes a writer readable.

If you aspire to be a writer, to have your words read by people who don't know you at all, then get into the habit of reading through what you have written as if you were someone else, asking yourself: "Does this interest me?" To every story there must be a beginning, a middle, and an end. In the beginning the reader's interest must be captured, in the middle it must be held, and at the end it must not flag, or die a drawn-out death. Ask yourself if you would have troubled to read your story right through, and be honest with your answer.

Writing is great fun, it is a wonderful hobby, but it is a two-sided affair, like acting on the stage. An actor doesn't act merely to amuse himself, but to entertain or amuse his audience. In the same way a writer who writes only for herself is making very little use of her craft. If you want to be appreciated by your reader, forestall criticism from others by finding fault with yourself. You can get infinite pleasure from writing as a hobby, you can give infinite pleasure to others by practising and trying to perfect whatever gift you have.

Practice makes for perfection, and the whole secret of good writing is enthusiasm and sincerity. Finally, if you aspire to turn your hobby to good account, remember the secret of success lies in applying the back of your skirt to the seat of your chair.

NOVICE COOK

Nella Whitfield

BEFORE ATTEMPTING TO "COOK by the book", the youthful novice in the kitchen will find it useful to know about the various—and most up-to-date—methods of cooking. She should also become acquainted with the meaning of the culinary terms likely to be encountered in cookery books. Simple basic recipes are not difficult to master, and will be her standby until such time as she can exercise her imagination and skill in devising more exciting and appetizing dishes.

METHODS OF COOKING

BAKING AND ROASTING. Roasting once meant cooking by radiant heat, and the terms were applied to meat cooked over, or in front of, an open fire. More usually, nowadays, they mean cooking in an oven heated by electricity, gas, oil, or solid fuel.

GRILLING AND BROILING. Grilling is a term commonly used in this country to describe cooking by the direct heat of a grill which has been heated until red-hot.

Food usually cooked by this means are: small cuts of meat (steaks, chops, rashers of bacon, etc.), portions of fish, or small whole ones (herrings, kippers, etc.), as well as the light browning of dishes coated with a sauce, grated cheese, etc.

In America this method of cooking as applied to meat, fish, poultry, or game, is described as "broiling", and not only does this describe cooking by deflected heat of gas or electric grill, etc., but cooking on a hot grid over, or in front of, a glowing and smokeless fire.

BOILING. This way of cooking is by the application of moist heat, the food to be cooked coming into contact with boiling water. It depends on the nature of the food to be cooked whether the water boils rapidly, moderately, or at simmering pace. A deep cooking-pan is used, which should be covered by a close-fitting lid, if evaporation of liquid is to be retarded.

STEWING. This term is applied to cooking gently in a saucepan, as above, over heat, or in a covered container in the oven. The object of cooking this way is to tenderize tough cuts of meat. This is a slower process of cooking than boiling.

FRYING. This means cooking food in heated fat or oil.

Shallow Frying means using very little fat or oil in the pan—usually a frying-pan.

Deep Frying (sometimes termed French frying) is to immerse the food to be cooked

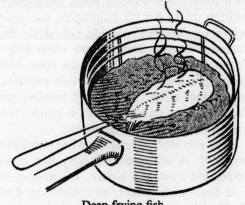

Deep frying fish.

in a deeper pan, in sufficient fat or oil to cover completely, and the latter must be heated to a certain temperature in order to seal in the juices of the food, at the same time preventing fat or oil soaking in and spoiling the food so cooked.

SAUTEING. A word derived from the French "sauter", meaning to toss. It is a process similar to frying in shallow fat, but has three objects—to cook completely in a *little* fat or oil, such foods as will cook fairly quickly—sliced kidneys, liver, par-boiled potatoes cut in slices or diced, etc.—tossing and shaking the pan in which they are cooked until the fat or oil is absorbed; as a preliminary step when preparing vegetables for soups and stews—sometimes sauces; or to complete cooking and add flavour and colour to certain dishes or their garnish—fried croûtons (pieces of bread), breadcrumbs, etc.

Some skill is required with all methods of frying to obtain good results—mainly dependent on heating the cooking fat or oil to the required temperatures for the food to be fried. With a thermometer this is easy and desirable for deep-fat frying. Without a thermometer, these tests will be a guide:

1. Cessation of spluttering (bubbles indicating that water is present and must evaporate before fat is ready to use for frying), with faint blue haze rising from surface of liquid fat or oil. Immerse food to be cooked without delay. If over-heated, the fat or oil will throw off a dense haze, indicating that it is scorching—and spoiling as a medium for cooking.

2. Throw a cube of bread into the heated fat or oil. If it causes some spluttering and becomes golden in one minute, the fat or oil is ready for cooking.

STEAMING. This is another method of cooking by moist heat. It is slower than boiling or stewing, because the food is cooked in the steam from boiling water. With this method there is less risk of over-cooking, and the flavour is considered better with less loss of vitamin values. The essential thing is to maintain the boiling point of the water over which the food is cooked, and for this purpose, the steamer must have a tightly-fitting lid.

PRESSURE-COOKING. This is a method of cooking by steaming under pressure. It is quicker than any other method of cooking, because the temperature is higher and sustained. Apart from time-saving, advantages are as above in relation to flavour and vitamin values.

TO CASSEROLE. To cook "en casserole" generally means cooking food (usually meats and vegetables) in a utensil called a casserole—a vessel with a close-fitting lid—in the oven. The advantages of this way of cooking are four-fold:

1. It saves dish-washing, because the casserole may be taken straight from the oven to the table, thereby eliminating any other cooking-pan (where the casserole contains a one-dish meal) or serving-dish.

2. The food requires no watching, and there is no loss in juices or appearance if the meal must be delayed for any reasonable length of time, ready for serving piping hot at any time.

3. A whole meal—meat, vegetables and gravy—can be cooked in one container on a shelf in the oven, leaving the remainder of the oven space free for other cooking.

4. Tough meats can be tenderized and vegetables prepared in a variety of ways and cooked without losing their valuable juices or flavours.

Originally, a casserole was a clay cooking-pot used commonly in France. Nowadays, it is made of a variety of materials—fireproof glass, vitreous china, earthenware, aluminium, and decorative ironware.

BRAISING. Means first browning meats or vegetables in a small quantity of hot fat, then adding a little liquid and cooking slowly in a covered container in the oven or over low top-stove heat.

POACHING. To cook small pieces of food —eggs, fillets or cutlets of fish, etc.—by slipping them into almost boiling (sometimes quite boiling) liquid to cover. More usually, a poached egg is an egg cooked in a greased container over steam until all white liquid sets round the yolk, which for general taste should not be cooked until firm.

SHIRRING. A term given to eggs cooked in cream or a purée of cooked vegetables, i.e. raw eggs broken into "nests" scooped in cooked spinach, then set in a moderately hot oven.

SCALLOPED. A method of cooking par-cooked or quickly cooked pieces of food in a fairly shallow dish—or individual dishes—first covering with a little sauce and/or breadcrumbs, etc.

WHIPPING OR WHISKING. Beating with a large fork or egg whisk to incorporate air and cause expansion in such foods as eggs, cream, half-set gelatin mixtures, etc.

MARINATING. Leaving food to soak in oil and vinegar—or vinegar alone.

BARBECUEING. Cooking food—usually whole animals or large joints of meat—slowly over direct heat, and basting at intervals with a highly seasoned sauce.

FRITTERING. Means coating small portions of food with a thick batter mixture, and cooking them in hot, deep fat.

SOUSING. Usually means cooking small whole fish—or fillets—in vinegar—or vinegar and water—and leaving them to "souse" until cold before eating.

BASIC RECIPES

SAUCES. If meat, bird or fish is really good, no sauce can improve on its flavour revealed by perfect cooking. Nevertheless, the making of sauces is an art—and not a difficult art at that, provided instructions are followed and the cook has a discriminating palate—and there are occasions when a well-made sauce can not only enhance a subtly flavoured dish, but transforms a food of indifferent quality—remnants of a previously cooked meal—or something out of a tin—into dishes that are a delight to eat. Sauce-making is an important branch of cooking.

WHITE FOUNDATION SAUCE. (To make $\frac{1}{2}$ pt. sauce.)
1 oz. butter or margarine, $\frac{3}{4}$ oz. plain flour, $\frac{1}{2}$ pt. white stock (liquor from boiling white meat and vegetables) or milk.

Melt the fat in a saucepan and add the flour, stirring with wooden spoon over very low heat until the mixture (known as a "roux") is smooth—about 3 minutes. Heat stock or milk and stir in gradually,

A meat pie made with rough-puff pastry.

mixing and cooking, but without actually boiling, until all liquid is absorbed smoothly. Now cook gently, stirring all the time, for 6 minutes. Until more experienced, the novice cook will find it easier to carry out this second stage of cooking (after liquid is added) in the upper compartment of a double cooker, when the cooking time should be at least 12–15 minutes. Another reason for recommending a double cooker is that the sauce is far less likely to catch at the bottom, or become lumpy should it be necessary to attend to some other dish being cooked at the same time, or to keep the sauce hot for a while. Adjust seasoning of sauce to taste, and add a small nut of butter, stirring until absorbed before serving.

The above is a sauce of pouring consistency. For a thinner sauce, add a little extra liquid. For a thicker coating sauce, use a little more flour—about 1 ounce.

To the foundation sauce may be added such solid ingredients as chopped parsley, chopped hard-boiled eggs, grated cheese, etc., depending on the dish with which it is to be served.

There are dozens of different kinds of sauces, and as experience grows the novice cook will be able to experiment with the white sauce foundation.

BROWN FOUNDATION SAUCE. This is made in the same way as white sauce, the main difference being that at the beginning the flour and fat are cooked together until they darken, making a brown "roux", using instead of light stock or milk, a brown stock or gravy. If when sufficiently cooked the sauce is not as brown as desired, a little liquid gravy browning (burnt sugar colouring) can be added. The flavourings will be determined by the meat or other essences in the stock or gravy, or any other additions deemed appropriate to the dish with which the sauce is served.

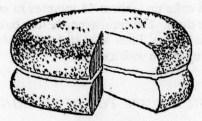
Sponge Cake.

CAKES. There are three basic methods of making cakes. "Rubbing in" of fats to flour until like fine breadcrumbs; "creaming" fat and sugar together until soft and light before adding the beaten eggs and folding in the flour; and the "whisking" of eggs first of all. There is a fourth class, to be tried when more experienced, whereby cakes—and biscuits—are made by less conventional methods that do not conform to any cake-making rule.

RECIPE FOR "RUBBING IN"

ROCK CAKES.
8 oz. self-raising flour, pinch salt, 3 oz. margarine, 3 oz. castor sugar, 1–2 eggs, 3–4 oz. dried fruit, grated rind ½ lemon, little milk, as required.

Sift flour with pinch salt. Cut in fat, then rub with finger-tips lightly and quickly, incorporating air by raising the hands up from the mixing bowl as you rub in the fat.

When mixture looks like fine breadcrumbs, sprinkle in the fruit and grated lemon rind. Beat egg (or eggs) and add with a little milk to make a *stiff* consistency. Using two forks, place small, rough heaps of mixture, spaced a little apart, on a greased baking sheet. Bake on top shelf of hot oven for 12–15 minutes, or until richly browned on the peaks. Oven temperature 450°F., Regulo mark 7–8.

Note. Use any other flavouring you like. If desired, bake mixture in a greased and

21

lined cake tin—about 45 minutes in *moderate* oven. The consistency before baking should be a little less stiff—drop from mixing spoon with a shake.

BASIC RECIPE FOR "CREAMING"

PLAIN CAKE MIXTURE.

2 eggs and their weight in each of the following ingredients—butter or margarine . . . castor sugar . . . self-raising flour (or plain flour and 1 small teaspoonful baking powder.)

Soften the fat in room temperature (not melt) and beat well with wooden spoon. Add the sugar and beat together until mixture is soft and lighter in colour. Beat eggs well and add gradually, beating well after each addition. (If liked, the eggs may be added unbeaten, but then you will need to beat the mixture longer.) Up to now every effort has been made to introduce air into the mixture by beating. Fold in flour, etc., *without beating* (or air will be driven out), adding any extra liquid required to make the mixture a soft one that will drop from the spoon with a slight shake. Put mixture into a greased and lined cake-tin—about 6 inch diameter—and bake in a moderate oven until firm when lightly pressed with finger-tips in the middle.

This recipe can be varied as you please —adding 2 tablespoonfuls desiccated coconut to make it a coconut cake; about 2 oz. halved or quartered glacé cherries to make it a cherry cake; or grated rind (outer zest) of lemon or orange, to make it a lemon or orange cake—or dried fruit, peel, or chopped nuts to make it a fruit cake, etc. The mixture may also be baked in small patty tins, or fancy paper cases—or on a shallow tin, greased and lined, and when cooked and cold, cut into shapes and iced and decorated to taste.

BASIC RECIPE FOR "WHISKING"

SPONGE CAKE MIXTURE.

2 eggs and their weight in fine castor sugar and flour (either self-raising, or plain flour with 1 small teaspoonful baking powder).

Prepare two 7-inch sandwich tins, by greasing with lard or cooking fat. Sift together 1 teaspoonful each of flour and fine castor sugar. Use this to sprinkle inside tins until fat is evenly covered.

Whisk eggs in a bowl, using an egg beater. Add sugar and whisk together well. Lodge mixing bowl over a saucepan containing hot water, and continue whisking over the steam until mixture is thick. (The bottom of the bowl should not rest in the hot water.) Remove bowl to table and fold in sifted flour, mixing smoothly without beating. Divide mixture between the two sandwich tins, and bake in hot oven for 8–10 minutes, or until sponge layers are well risen and firm to the touch. Turn out on to wire tray and leave until cool before sandwiching layers together with jam, cream, etc.

Note. Any flavourings should be added whilst whisking eggs and sugar together.

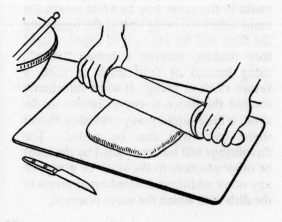

PASTRY-MAKING

SHORT CRUST. This is the easiest pastry of all provided the rules of making are followed closely:

Basic recipe—8 oz. plain flour, 4 oz. fat (a mixture of margarine and lard or cooking fat will give excellent results), a little cold water.

For savoury pastry—add a pinch of salt to the flour when sifting.

For sweet pastry—add 1 teaspoonful *fine castor* sugar, instead of salt.

Sift flour, etc., into a large bowl. Cut in the fat with a knife until pieces are small, then rub in lightly with finger-tips, lifting the hands high above the bowl to introduce air. When ingredients are like fine crumbs, moisten with cold water sparingly—using just sufficient to bind. If too much water is used, the pastry dough will be sticky to handle, and heavy when cooked.

Dredge a little flour over the pastry board and lightly flour the rolling pin. Then roll out pastry until of required thickness.

For pies (single crust). To prevent pastry sinking, fill pie-dish well, setting a pie-funnel in the middle to hold up the crust and prevent it getting soggy.

Glossy finish. Brush pastry sparingly with beaten egg or egg and milk, *before* baking.

Sugary finish. Brush lightly with water and sprinkle liberally with castor sugar *before* baking. For a crisp, sugary finish, smear pastry *when almost cooked* with beaten white of egg followed by sprinkling of castor sugar. Return to oven to finish cooking. Oven heat—hot—about 450°F., or Regulo mark 7.

To "flute" pie pastry edges, place first finger and thumb (about ½ inch apart) close to edges, and firmly pinch up at even distances apart.

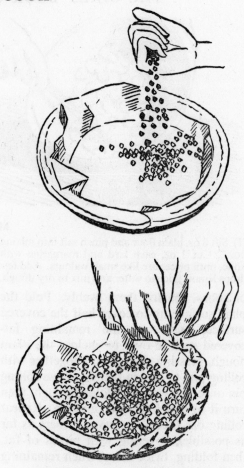

Baking pastry cases "blind". Put grease-proof paper at the bottom of the pastry case and cover with a layer of dried beans.

For decorative ventilation (to allow steam to escape), make a series of inch-long slashes with sharp knife radiating from centre where pie-funnel protrudes.

FLAKY PASTRY. Make a richer pastry than for short crust, allowing 6 oz. fat to 8 oz. flour. Divide fat into four parts, and rub in one part to the flour, etc. Moisten with cold water and a half-teaspoonful lemon juice, until dough is soft and elastic. (A little more moisture is required than for short pastry.) Roll out on floured board to a neat *oblong* shape—much longer than wide. On two-thirds of pastry surface place another portion of fat cut into pieces

23

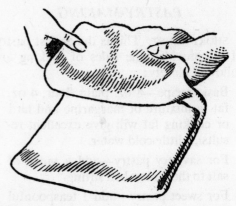

MINCE PIES

(1) Sift 8 oz. plain flour and pinch salt into mixing bowl. Cut 3 oz. each lard and margarine with knife, until pieces are like small walnuts. Add few drops lemon juice to water and mix to dry dough.

(2) Knead dough lightly into a ball. Then roll out to an oblong. Fold into three, sealing edges with rolling pin. Turn folded edges to one side and roll out again.

or cubes, spacing them evenly. Fold the plain surface up to cover half the covered surface, and turn the remaining fat-covered surface over to enclose the plain dough, pressing edges firmly together with rolling pin, to seal in the air. Press rolling pin once or twice over folded dough, then turn it so that fold is to one side. Repeat rolling out (keeping square corners as far as possible), covering with pieces of fat, then folding, twice more, when remaining

fat will have been used up. Between each stage, leave pastry to "rest" (about 20 minutes). As with short pastry, use the rolling pin with short, light forward movements, taking care that the fat does not pierce the dough. This will be easy if you first blend the fats, mixing them with a fork until they are of a similar softness to the dough. Turn fold to same side each time.

Flaky pastry should be baked in a hot-

(3) Repeat folding, rolling and turning to one side three or four times. Cut into medium-size circles with plain cutter. On half of these put mincemeat. Brush edges of remaining circles with water.

(4) Place one circle over each mound of mincemeat, pressing edges firmly together. Arrange on baking sheet and pierce tops with skewer. Bake for 20 minutes in hot oven. Above quantities make 18 mince pies.

ter oven than for short pastry—about 500°F., Regulo mark 9.

ROUGH PUFF PASTRY. Use the same proportions as for flaky pastry. Sift flour, etc., into a mixing bowl, and cut in fat to the size of walnuts. Bind ingredients with cold water and a little lemon juice to make a stiff dough. Roll out on floured board to an oblong, as for flaky pastry, keeping squared corners. Fold top edges to centre, then bring up bottom edges to top fold. Give pastry a half turn to one side (as for flaky pastry) and press once or twice with rolling pin over surface. Place dough in a cold place—a refrigerator, if you have one —for 20 minutes. Repeat rolling, folding, etc., a further three times before rolling out and using as required. Keep board and rolling pin lightly dusted with flour to prevent sticking at any stage. Oven temperature as for flaky pastry.

PUFF PASTRY. This is the most difficult pastry of all—it takes longer and requires more precision when rolling out to ensure even paper-thin layers of pastry. This pastry is usually used for making "vol-au-vent" dishes.

Allow the same weight of fat as flour. Sprinkle a little salt with the flour and sift twice. If possible, use butter for flavour, though margarine is a good substitute.

Rub in one ounce of fat into sifted flour, etc., and mix with water containing a few drops of lemon juice, to a dough of similar consistency to the fat. Give the dough a little light kneading to ensure evenness of moisture, then roll out to an oblong three times its width. Roll out fat between the folds of floured muslin—or greaseproof paper—to a size of even thickness that will cover one-third of the area of the dough, one inch from the edges. Place fat in middle of dough, then fold first one end (nearest), then the other end over, pressing

edges lightly but firmly with rolling pin. Turn dough, keeping open end nearest. This process of rolling out, folding and turning must be repeated 7 times in all, allowing a "rest" between each process of about 20 minutes, leaving pastry covered with a piece of muslin or folded greaseproof paper.

To make "vol-au-vent", or puff pastry cases, roll out prepared dough to slightly more than ¼-inch thickness. For small cases, cut into rounds with a fluted cutter the size of a tumbler, then use a smaller cutter to mark *half-way* through each, taking care not to cut right through. Use larger cutters for "vol-au-vent", depending on size required.

As for other rich pastry, the oven for puff pastry must be hot—500°F., or Regulo mark 9–10. The baking time will be from 20–30 minutes. To glaze, remove pastry from oven just before it is quite cooked, and brush over with a little egg, or egg yolk and milk, returning it to the oven until nicely browned and glossy. When cooked, lift pastry "lids" and carefully scoop out the soft paste. When required,

Pride in the young cook's first attempt at Roast Chicken.

fill with savoury or sweet filling and re-place "lids", tilted to show filling.

GENERAL HINTS

To bake pastry cases "blind" means to bake them without any filling mixture, and short pastry is often cooked this way. To prevent any rising or "bubbling" whilst cooking, first prick the pastry all over at the bottom of the case—or put a piece of greaseproof paper at the bottom and cover with a layer of dried beans or rice, etc., removing when the pastry cases are almost cooked and returning them to the oven to finish cooking. The same beans, etc., may be used repeatedly.

Flan cases are more crisp-eating when made of "biscuit" pastry—short pastry ingredients moistened with just sufficient egg yolk beaten with a little cold water, to bind. Sometimes this is referred to as "fleur" pastry.

It is not necessary to grease tins in, or on which, pastry is cooked—unless any recipe specially states this should be done.

To ensure crispness, always remove pastry from cooking tin, and when cool do *not* store in an airtight tin, but in a cool larder. Exceptions—double-crust pies or tarts cooked with a moist filling on a heat-proof plate. If moved they might break.

WAYS WITH FLOWERS

Peggy Scott

MOST GIRLS HAVE AN URGE to create beauty, either in them-selves—their clothes, attention to hygiene and skin care, or in their immediate sur-roundings—or in a wider field: through

beautiful embroidery, drawings, paintings, and so on.

A never-ending source of pleasure is a hobby with flowers. If you have tried painting pictures and have found that you

A tall vase containing irises, tulips, carnations and hyacinths and asparagus foliage.

Photo by courtesy of Longmans Ltd.

27

have no talent (or patience?) for this, try making "pictures" with flower arrangements instead. They won't last as long, of course, but they will give pleasure to you and others—and, in time, you can develop a talent for unusual flower arrangement that can well lead to a well-paid career.

Flowers are always wanted, for private and public functions, and any girl with a flair for arranging them artistically can turn this hobby into money—or just go on enjoying the job for its own sake, all through her life.

Before you begin, study flower paintings for line and colour and contrast. You can buy picture postcards of Flemish or Dutch flower pictures, at any art shop.

Then try a simple arrangement—mixed flowers which even a small garden can produce. Don't use a *glass* vase until you are more experienced in cleverly arranging only a few special flowers or one beautiful bloom with an attractive, graceful stem. A glass vase or bowl shows up the massed stems of mixed flowers, dirty water, and the flower-holder, and so spoils your "picture".

A holder is necessary for placing stems at angles. Tall vases need the wire-netting (with large mesh) type of holder. Crumple it, push it into the vase and hook it just inside, so that it can be hidden by a flower or leaf.

If you use shallow vases, the netting should be tied inside with string or fine wire—as you would tie a parcel. This is better than other kinds of holders, which tend to make flowers stand up too stiffly.

Now start building. Put in the large flowers or branches first; then the centre one, and gradually add the rest.

Taking care of flowers

Plunge your flowers up to their necks in fresh water for an hour before you start arranging. Keep them in a cool, dark place, if possible. Strip the foliage from stems, and also any fine shoots which steal the water from the flowers.

The best vases are those which hold sufficient water at the drinking point: that is, the end of the stalk. The vases should not be so slim that flowers which take up a lot of water are dry and thirsty in a short time.

If you have made an elaborate arrangement, which you do not want to disturb, fill up the water in the vase. It is not necessary to change it regularly except for flowers like wallflowers, stocks, etc., which become slimy and give the water an unpleasant smell.

Cut the stalks, because the tips will have dried (in the case of bought flowers) in transit. Cut the ends of rose stems with a sharp knife, slantwise, before putting them into water—and remove some alternate leaves from the stems.

Hammer the ends of hard-wooded stalks like chrysanthemums, and remove some of the leaves—or cut up the centre for two or three inches from the end.

You can also bruise the stems of flowers with woody stalks, or of branches of foliage, so that they will last longer.

Change the water as required—and shorten the stalks each time before re-arranging.

Unusual arrangements

When flowers are scarce, you can look to the autumn or winter hedgerows for inspiration. Use your imagination and mix bare branches (choose those with the most graceful lines) with berries, such as rose hips or blackberries; crab-apples; even vegetable leaves if you are certain that they will blend, in shape and colour, with the rest.

Placing the flower arrangement

Low bowls of simple, mixed flowers look well on broad window-sills or low

An arrangement of June flowers, which include carnations, delphiniums, stocks, irises, and ixia.

Photo by courtesy of Longmans Ltd.

Small roses or marguerite heads make a lovely bracelet.

A coronet or spray across top of head, with short hairstyle.

Below: A bunch of violets at the throat.

side-tables; bigger, wider vases containing larger, more brilliant flowers, against a plain wall; tall vases, holding cherry or apple blossom, or mixed foliage, on a polished floor, on an antique coffer, or in a fireplace. *Always keep the background simple.*

Once started, you can go on creating beauty with flowers all the year round—and you can add to your own adornment, too!

Flowers for yourself

American girls, who are famous for their smart and feminine appearance, love wearing flowers, even at work. It is a charming custom and I should like to see it adopted in our own country. It gives one a "lift" for the day—and it certainly cheers up people who meet the wearer! It needs only a little thought and ingenuity, so why let our American cousins have *all* the credit for glamour?

Here are a few ideas for arranging your own posies—and where to wear them for special occasions.

For daytime

A small bunch of violets or a rose at the throat; a few sprigs of lavender or a gay anemone tucked into the band of a plain hat; two bunches of violets or forget-me-nots pushed into your belt (at the front, or side—or even at the back).

Then try a single flower pinned on the revers of your suit jacket—or a small mixed bunch of simple garden flowers, or lily of the valley, pushed into your top pocket.

For evening wear

Avoid orchids, which are for your older, more sophisticated sister. *Yours* should be sweet young flowers (such as those mentioned above): tiny roses, posies, or a single delphinium floret, can be fixed to ear-clips to give lovely floral ear-rings.

A simple jug arrangement: carnations, irises, gladioli, double white narcissi and beech foliage.

Photo by courtesy of Longmans Ltd.

31

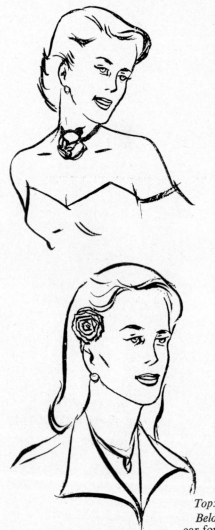

Even bracelets can be made with fresh flowers. Use pansies or small flowers, such as small roses, forget-me-nots—or marguerite heads—depending on the colour of your party dress.

Sew them carefully on velvet ribbon—or use elastic thread to run through large flower-heads such as marguerites.

Flowers in the hair always look attractive. Try different arrangements to suit the shape of your face and your hair-style. Long hair needs something at one side; short hair either a coronet or a spray across the top-centre.

Try a single flower behind the ear, in the nape of the neck—or a spray clustered round a top-knot. If you cling to a horse-tail style, then tuck a posy into your ribbon at the back.

Daisies, marguerites, camellias, cornflowers—almost any kind of "young" flower that matches or contrasts with your dress—will do.

The girl who loves flowers—and is there one who doesn't?—will have endless delight in a hobby which gives pleasure both to herself and countless others. Flowers, which are for ever creating beauty themselves, simply ask you to continue their job!

Top: A rose on velvet neck-band for party wear.
Below: A single flower at one side, tucked behind one ear for long hair style.

PAINT YOUR OWN PICTURE

Odette Tchernine

WE ARE ALL BORN WITH THE intuition of some form of art or creative ability within us. It differs according to what sort of person each one of us happens to be.

The gift is often not realized by you who possess it, and then sign-posts are a great help. They open your eyes to what quality lies in you to develop.

When I was only three I used to amuse myself drawing the Brighton fishing fleet from our first-floor balcony. Just to test me, my mother once remarked: "Why have you drawn such big boats and then such small ones? Don't you remember we saw them last Friday aground near the fish market, and they were all the same, not big and small like these!"

I gave my mother a look of affectionate derision, I was told in later years, and with infinite patience I explained: "Really, Mummy, can't you see? Some boats are small in my picture because they are far away, and not so near the beach as the big ones."

Quite naturally in my baby mind, I had worked out the technique of perspective, because it happened to be in me, as it may be in you, to observe such things.

One child, for instance, may have a quick, retentive ear for music, and will sing a melody from memory after one hearing, while another thinks she is humming a popular tune quite correctly, but the poor pet is actually hopping about to an unrecognizable set of notes. And she is not aware that there is no music in her, for she is insensitive to sound.

Sensitivity, whether to sound or to design or colour, can be stimulated, woken up.

That is what I am going to try to do in this article for your so far untried drawing and painting. And you will no doubt find it useful, even if you already have found out something about art.

Most of you have had some varied degree of drawing lessons at school. You may have done a little experimental sketching, and own a box of students' water-colours. Take out your materials, and make a short inventory. As I do not know what you have to make a start, I shall begin from scratch, and suggest the tools for your study. Your interest may be for pleasure, or it may be because you might make use of your talent later on in your work.

Whatever your aims, these sign-posts can help.

Buy a sketch-book, two if possible. One should be pocket-size for handiness, and the other rather larger, as it is always better to start practising drawing on a broad,

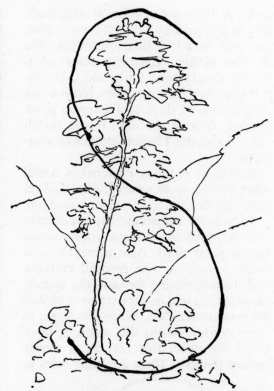

The chief points of interest come within the design of the imaginary S standing up.

free scale. You can always reduce your drawing when you have had more practice, but to begin sketching too much on a miniature scale cramps the style. Sketch-books on those spiral-wire hinges where you can tear out any sheet, are a good idea. The paper should be of the cartridge variety, which is quite cheap, or should be medium-grained artist's paper. Art paper varies in texture. The rough kind is good for quick, broad effects, like wild seas, or stormy skies, whether for black and white work, or for water-colour painting. The smoother variety helps a clear defining of outlines, and attains a smooth glow and transparency of colour, if you are painting delicate flowers, birds, or butterflies.

Next, you choose your pencils. Get a 4B or 3B. They are of medium consistence, neither too hard nor too soft, and quite dark. A large india-rubber is suggested, for you will work by trial and error at first, and even for a long time afterwards. We do that always. Learning never ends. Pencils should have fairly short, stubby points, or they break too often, but you can sharpen one of them to a thinnish point for fine, delicate shading. If you sketch out of doors, don't forget penknife or sharpener.

French or ordinary charcoal is useful when you get more assured; fine, bold results can be obtained from that medium.

To find your subject matter, first observe your surroundings. It is not always necessary to go far afield. An ornament in your room, a window with graceful curtains, and the sun shining through, the homely tea-kettle, glasses, or cups are good objects for primary practice. When you begin to draw still life, or any life, scene, or landscape, remember that nothing is merely surface flatness. There are other sides to it, even if they are invisible to you from your observation point.

Begin by copying in outline what you see. Then imagine your model in all its contours, sides, back, beneath. Then make another drawing of it, still outlining just what you see, but now putting in shadings and under-shadows and curves that denote those other dimensions. Such is the meaning of accurate design, and "implication" in form; the avoiding of that effect of flatness as if an outline was just cut out from cardboard and had nothing else to it.

When you are drawing, whether your model is a bunch of flowers, a tree, or a landscape, never work in straight, continuous lines. Nature is not like that. Much can be learnt, by studying a scene, and taking it to pieces with your understanding as well as your eyes. You must be the wanderer walking in the picture to make it real. You must be the seed that began the miraculous flower in all its petals and

Each point of interest comes within the design of an imaginary S lying on its back.

stamens to understand the wonder of its true reproduction through the medium of your art.

In the landscape, you will see strong, yet curved, irregular strokes nearest to you, on the ground, on ridges, on tree trunks and boughs. The house shadows will be quite heavy in the foreground, but the wee hut on the other side of the river or pond has a softer contour, and its shade is less pronounced. So your physical and mental eye travels ahead until it reaches the final spot artists call vanishing-point. That is the farthest horizon: the end of a village road where it bends around a far corner, the low clouds where the sky seems like a faint, smudgy bowl, the rim of the sea where it appears to end like a ruled line. But never draw it like an actual ruled line. It is softer than that.

The beginner should start with outlines only. Suppose you are on a rocky beach, and there is not a boat or seagull asking to be drawn. Try one of the rocks. First the contours, irregular, jagged, sometimes curved as well. Then section it out as it appears to you. Shade in the hollows, the recesses and cracks. You can experiment in a complete grading of light and shade by pencilling in your shadow lines, softly, close together, darkly and shoulder to shoulder, as it were, or spaced out to give an illusion of light on the stone. Shade your strokes in different directions for contrast. Those principles can be applied to any drawing. Always handle your pencil lightly. It is safer to go over an outline or a shadow twice, than to have made it too strong in the first place.

From black and white drawing, the next step is to try your hand at water-colour versions of your experiments.

First of all, let me say this: To draw or paint a nature scene on the spot is ideal, but it is not entirely necessary to return there again and again until you have finished a precise and painstaking record. It can never be an absolutely reliable record in every detail anyhow, because nature and atmosphere are always altering. If detailed accuracy is wanted, then I will say, pack up those water-colours, and instead learn colour photography.

In water-colours, impression is the aim. The looker-on recognizes a scene in your picture by the general impression received, not by your sketching in the numerically correct number of trees in a favourite valley.

Some of the greatest artists have painted from memory, so you need not feel at a disadvantage if the British climate allows you to study a beautiful landscape in perfect mood only once, and then decrees that you must trust to what you remember of it to create an enlarged or more finished painting based on a quick, rough sketch executed when you were actually there.

I often make rapid drawings of scenes that appeal to me, work in some indications in coloured chalks, or even scribble colour reminders on different spots in the sketch. Then I develop the painting later. I have even got some quite successful impressions from a fleeting train window.

All that helps to develop your colour memory and your sense of design.

The student can get quite good practice by copying snapshots of pleasing scenes and places, counting on her memory and taste in design to help her eliminate too much detail that might make a copy inartistic.

Elimination of unnecessary detail is an important factor. The true artist does not paint in each visible leaf or twig. Broader effects are best, allied with correct strength or dilution in colour. Follow the ruling I suggested for black and white drawing: strong colour in the foreground, less in the middle distance, and fainter still as it fades to the horizon.

This example suggests the balanced dispersal of points of interest, and the correct unequal division between sea and sky. Note that the sailing boat is not exactly in centre of picture.

Your water-colour requirements will be these: One good-sized sable-hair brush which will be quite expensive but which with care will last for years. Always wash paint out of brushes in warm water with a little soap, rinse, and keep away from dust. Two more brushes, slightly smaller, one quite small, are required if you ever do flowers, birds, or insects in miniature pictures.

Your drawing sketch books will do for colour work as well as for black and white. Get colours in tubes. They do not dry up so quickly as in the little pans. Some advisers consider scholars' paints good enough for beginners. I do not. Get fewer paints, but get good-quality artists' colours. They do not fade, and you will be rewarded if quite by chance one of your first efforts should turn out surprisingly effective. It does happen occasion-

ally, this strange thing that my art master used to call "An accident of the hand".

The primary, basic colours to buy first are: vermilion red, ultramarine and cobalt blues, crimson lake, cadmium yellow, which is so much clearer and better value than ordinary yellow chrome. Then get sepia brown. From such colours the novice obtains any necessary hues for first attempts. Blue and yellow mixed produces green, a wisp of sepia dulls it when required. Crimson lake and any of the blues produces violet, mauve, or purple according to proportions mixed. Crimson lake and yellow make a flame shade, and orange is produced by marrying vermilion red to yellow. Do not ever use sepia too strongly, for it is a powerful colour, and a little goes a long way. When painting an autumn scene, sepia tones down orange, yellow, and gold if too strong. A very lovely and satisfying grey is got by mingling vermilion red and ultramarine blue. Chinese white is seldom used in true, pure water-colour. It is what is known as a "body colour", and exists for application in very special cases. Some artists do mix it in with other colours to obtain a velvety texture in their painting, but it is heavy-looking, and not really good.

Effects for flowers, sunshine, light, or sea foam do not require Chinese white. For that you employ the technique of leaving some of the white paper untouched. The technique requires some study, but it is attractive, light and delicate when mastered.

Grained paper is best, as with black and white drawing, for doing seas, forests and anything wild and rugged. For delicate flowers the smoother paper is recommended. It combines its own soft texture with the lightness of touch required, and gives a velvety finish and bloom to the subject.

As you progress, here are some other lovely colours that are useful and go a long way because of their intensity: Viridian green, scarlet lake, burnt sienna, Vandyke brown, and yellow ochre. There is a deep ochre too which gives rich tones. The paint box should always have black in it, though for sparing use. If you get some, buy ivory black. It has a certain quality about it that makes it less heavy and dense to handle than lamp black.

Sometimes it is advisable to use the pure colour on your brush straight out of the tube, moistening the tip of the brush in your bowl of clean water. A white china saucer will do for setting out your different little blobs of pure colour that you think you will require. Have them all ready, because water-colour painting is quick work, and you cannot linger or the effect is lost.

There are no strict rules in painting. You learn your own tendencies, correct your faults, and try out different methods of application, for there are so many different styles. Always begin your sky first. Never divide your landscape in two equal halves, as that cuts the interest. The proportions should be three-quarters land and one-quarter sky, or the other way round.

One word of warning. Don't attempt an almost all-sky painting right away. It is very difficult.

Any tint the chosen scene demands may be washed in. You damp the paper first. Never put a colour over another until the first one is dry. It is, in fact, best to wash in your colours as you intend them to be right away; add very little to a blob of colour except perhaps a little darker accenting for shadows or hollows, or the thicker part of foliage on a tree. Always let the light show through tree branches. Do not paint them opaque. Use several shades of green, brown, darkish blue and grey for foliage and work broadly, letting colours mingle sometimes, without little finicky touches. Lovely skies and distant hill impressions are obtained too by washing in different desired colours and directing them to run together when wet.

Have clean blotting-paper handy to control those running rills of light and shade. Remember that impression of light and sparkle derives from leaving in some specks of the white paper unpainted. Work in your horizon lines rapidly as you want them, and then soften them.

I spoke of design a little farther back. That is the first step to an acceptable picture. Many artists do not use pencil but only wash in sparse indications in pale grey water-colour, but you have to be very sure for that, as it cannot rub out, so I advise pencil for a start. Use the minimum of light strokes. Bear in mind what I remarked about natural outlines. They should look as if there was a feeling of flexibility and movement here and there.

Nature always curves, retracts, or in the case of mountain peaks and crags, zigzags. When you compose your picture the design should form an imaginary S or Z across the paper or drawing-board. The S should be lying on its back if the picture is wider than high, and imagined as standing in its usual alphabetical posture if the picture is to be high and narrow—the sort of shape of paper you would use if you were sketching one tall Highland pine-tree, for instance. Incidents in the picture,

that is points of interest, should be evenly balanced within that imaginary design. They must not crowd in one corner, or all in the centre. That framework of the letter S helps the beginner to build up the design.

One last thought. Do visit the art galleries, and compare the great Masters of the past one with the other. Study the famous Moderns too, and try to understand that everything artists see is not only with their visible eye.

MAKE YOUR OWN JEWELLERY

Peggy Tearle

ONE OF THE MOST REWARDING of hobbies is the making of costume jewellery; only the simplest of tools and materials are needed and the craft is well within the scope of anyone able to sew. For the girl who—with little time or money to spare and no special qualification—would like to try her hand at designing and making her own jewellery, this simple method is ideal.

Sewing materials, beeswax, wire cutters, and a pair of small round-nosed pliers are the only tools required, while materials consist of hardware (curtain rings, S hooks, washers, chain), dressmaker accessories (jewels, beads, pearls, sequins), handicraft materials (metal studs, clasps, mounts) and various oddments, such as decorative buttons, old necklaces, dress trimmings, etc.

Brooches and ear-rings can be made on two-piece mounts, the front pieces of which are perforated; the ornament is sewn or wired to the front, after which the two pieces are joined by pressing down three metal flanges.

The following examples illustrate some

of the ways in which these simple materials can be converted into jewellery—no piece costing more than a shilling or two. As new ideas for designs will probably present themselves while you are making up this jewellery, keep tweezers and a little heap of mixed materials to hand, and play about with them; the game is fascinating and will teach you quite a lot about design.

When designing, resist the temptation to over-elaborate; choose materials in true jewel and metal colours and use them sparingly. Simple combinations of pattern and colour will produce the best designs.

GILT BROOCH AND EAR-RINGS

One round two-piece brooch mount, 1 inch diameter.

One pair two-piece ear-ring mounts, $\frac{5}{8}$ inch diameter.

Three round gilt studs, $\frac{3}{8}$–$\frac{1}{2}$ inch diameter.

Three hollow brass curtain rings to fit exactly round the studs.

One dozen round gilt studs, $\frac{1}{4}$ inch diameter.

Fine brass wire (such as one strand of twisted picture wire).

Durofix.

Brooch

Fix a large stud to the centre of the mount; if necessary enlarge the holes in the mount with a metal skewer or the point of a pair of compasses. Frame the stud with a curtain ring, couched down with three equidistant wire "stitches". (A short length of wire should be threaded through the mount, taken over the ring, and returned to the starting point—the two ends then twisted together at the back). Secure by twisting the three double wires together, and trim off the long ends.

Now enlarge alternate holes round the edge of the mount, making twelve large holes—each big enough to take two adjacent stud prongs. With pliers, give each of the small studs a little pinch—to bring the prongs closer together and make the tops slightly oval—then fix the twelve studs round the edge of the mount.

Having made sure that all prongs and wires are neatly flattened at the back, apply a coat of glue; then join the two pieces of the mount by pressing down the flanges with the side of a pair of pliers.

Ear-rings

Fix a large stud to the centre of the mount and frame with a curtain ring as for the brooch. Before joining front and back of ear-ring mounts, turn down two of the flanges and open the third out flat; the front will then slide in position, leaving only one flange to be dealt with after assembling.

Metal jewellery will not tarnish if a coat of lacquer is painted on. First clean with a silver cloth (brass polish may take the colour out of gilt and should be avoided) and finish by polishing with whiting; then apply the lacquer as quickly as possible. As lacquer is inflammable it should never be warmed or used near a flame, and the bottle should always be corked after use.

AMETHYST AND PASTE SET

One round two-piece brooch mount, 1 inch diameter.

One pair two-piece ear-ring mounts, $\frac{5}{8}$ inch diameter.

One round jewel, $\frac{5}{8}$ inch diameter

Two round jewels, $\frac{3}{8}$ inch diameter (amethyst or any jewel colour).

Fifteen large paste "sew-ons"

Twenty small paste "sew-ons" (sometimes called studs. Made in three sizes only).

One packet very small steel beads.

Brooch

Wax a double strand of pure silk thread and knot to the perforated piece of the mount, leaving a spare end of thread hanging loose. Fix on the large jewel with two small beads (the thread is taken through each of the holes of the jewel in turn, a bead threaded on and the needle returned to the starting point). Now bring the thread to the front, join on sufficient small beads to surround the jewel, form a circle by taking the thread twice through the first bead, and secure by couching to the mount. Next thread on the fifteen large paste stones round the edge, making a circle as before; then work all round the brooch, taking the thread through the second channel of each setting.

Knot and glue the ends of thread at the back of the mount, join front and back, and finish by running a little glue under the settings round the edge.

Ear-rings

Join a small jewel to the centre of the mount and surround with ten small paste stones, as described for the brooch.

When making this jewellery, be sure to keep the thread well waxed and avoid loose stitches, or loops, round the flanges of the mount. Frequent backstitching will help to keep the thread tight and ensure a firm professional finish.

GILT NECKLACE, BRACELET AND EAR-RINGS

Eighteen inches "½ inch oval" brass hardware chain.
Three dozen brass centre-pin domes.
One pair gilt ear-ring fittings (with ring, for drops).
Two large split rings.
Two small split rings.
Two clasps.

This set consists of single links of chain joined with domes. The domes (hollow-headed studs with split pins) are normally used either for handbag making or belt decoration, but can be converted into attractive links and pendants by shaping the pins with pliers. Large brass paper fasteners can be used in a similar way.

First try making some links as described here. If you have never handled pliers, it is worth while putting in a little practice; working step by step and following the diagrams, you will soon acquire the knack.

The pins of the dome are first opened out flat, then bent back over the edge of the stud, cut to the required length (A) and, working from the ends backwards, shaped into open loops, or shanks (B). The shanks are closed by pinching with pliers. To make a pendant dome, shape one pin only, cutting the other off at the base.

Diagrams A and B.

Necklace

Cut and remove alternate links of chain, leaving fifteen whole separate links; then join them with dome links. Attach the clasp, using a large split ring if necessary, and finish by hanging seven pendant domes from the central chain links.

Bracelet

Work as for the necklace, using seven of each type of link and omitting the pendants.

Ear-rings

Open the rings on the fitting by twisting the ends sideways from each other (do not pull them apart and spoil the shape of the ring); then hang a pendant dome from each one.

Stockists

For jewels, paste, gilt studs, mounts: A. Darnley Ltd., 18 Princes Street, Cavendish Square, London, W.1.

For centre-pin domes: Rowes Wool Shop, Leicester.

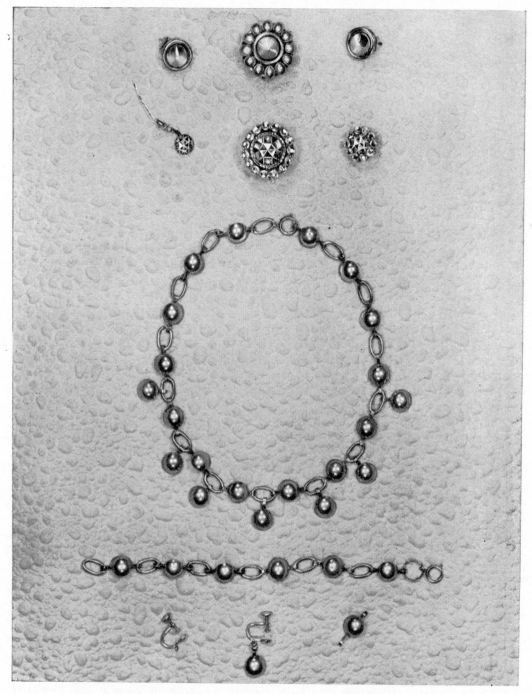

Some delightful ornaments you can make yourself.

Top, gilt brooch and ear-rings; *below*, amethyst and paste set; *centre*, gilt necklace, bracelet and ear-rings.

POTTERY AS A HOBBY

Jess M. Baker

POTTERY IS ONE OF THE VERY oldest of crafts. It originated in the East, in countries like Persia and China, Korea, and Japan. There are records of potters' wheels having been in existence as far back as 2000 B.C. and, even before then, pots were made by taking strips of clay and coiling them round, one above the other, rather after the style of basket-making. From that day to this, people the world over (from about the age of two upwards!) have been fascinated by this ancient craft of making from raw clay all sorts of shapes—jugs, bowls, beakers, vases, etc—which, when glazed and fired at a high temperature, become what we know as pottery.

In Japan there are potters in every small village, and the children like nothing better than going out and finding their own clay and building little kilns and trying, quite sucessfully, to imitate their elders at making pots. In the Western countries, pottery is not quite such a basic part of everyday life, but there has, in recent years, been a significant increase of interest in the craft. Perhaps it is partly because there is a general reaction against the tendency in the world today towards mass production of things that all look exactly alike. For, one of the beauties of making pottery is that every pot seems to have a character of its own.

How would *you* like to make pots? It really is fascinating. Have you ever held a piece of raw clay in your hands? It is a lovely material to handle, very plastic and easy to mould into different shapes. But that isn't pottery, of course. Pottery is the combination of raw clay and the spinning potter's wheel—or, rather, the art of your hands combining the clay and the movement to produce a shape.

Have you ever watched a potter at work? Quite often you can see one at some local exhibition—or, if there is a pottery in your district, it is well worth asking if you can be shown round. Alternatively, the Central Office of Information has made one or two industrial films in which pottery-making is shown—perhaps your local film society can be persuaded to show these?

I mention these aspects, because, as with all hobbies, the more you can find out about pottery, the more keen you will become to acquire efficiency at this old, yet ever exciting craft. I know when I first became interested in pottery, and someone took me to see an exhibition of Chinese pottery—of the T'ang and Sung periods —I got quite a new outlook on pottery from gazing at those wonderful, delicate bowls and bottles which, although made for use, were objects of beauty in themselves.

So I hope that you, too, if you are going to make it your hobby, will take the widest possible interest in pottery. Go to modern exhibitions. Read books and magazines about pottery. Above all, try to visit a few potteries; both hand-made potteries—such as those in Devon and Cornwall (there are several in London, too)—and the big potteries of Stoke-on-Trent, where literally thousands of people are employed.

In this way you may find a great deal more satisfaction from your hobby than if you just plodded along on your own.

But, you will want to know, how do I *start*? Well, that's simple enough. You must find a teacher. There are quite a few grammar schools which now include pottery as part of their art curriculum, but it it not a general practice, and you will probably have to attend classes at your local art school or technical college. If you make inquiries from your local educational authorities, they will put you in touch with the nearest establishment.

As a beginning, then, go along to the nearest art school or technical college and sign on for the part-time class in pottery. The cost is about 7s. 6d. for a whole year —that is, only 2s. 6d. per term of 13 weeks, with two classes a week. For this trifling sum, you will receive tuition from an expert pottery teacher, and all materials and tools are provided free. You can even, later on, buy for yourself, at a very small sum (6d. to 1s.) any of the pots you have made ("thrown" is the term).

Probably the first thing your instructor will teach you is how to knead the clay. This is the same sort of procedure as kneading bread, but done for the opposite reason—you knead clay to get all the air *out*. This makes the clay ready for "throwing".

Next, you will sit on the potter's wheel —at most art schools there are two or three of these. The wheel is rather like a circular bread board, sometimes made of wood and sometimes of stone. It is operated by kicking a bar with one foot continuously, causing the wheel to rotate in an anti-clockwise direction.

Your instructor will then place a rolled ball of clay in the centre of the wheel and explain to you the first and most important operation—namely, centring the clay. This consists of forming the lump into a

The author—Jess Baker—at work in her own pottery in Cornwall.

perfect cylinder, flattened at the top, and lying dead in the centre of the wheel while it is spinning round.

This sounds easy, but it will probably take you several lessons before you can accomplish this single feat. But take heart, for it is a basic and important first step. Once you have mastered centring, then you will find the subsequent processes of raising the clay and shaping it very much simpler.

Having "thrown" your very first pot, you will slice the bottom away from the wheel with a length of wire (rather as your grocer cuts a piece of cheese). Then, picking it up gently between the palms of your hands you place it on a shelf and leave it to dry.

Your pot is far from finished, however! When it is dry enough, you will be taught how to "slip" the pot—that is, dip it into an undercovering material, so that it is ready for "biscuiting". This means it is put in a kiln—a sort of brick oven heated by electric elements—and fired up to a

After you have mastered the art of centring the clay, you will find it easy to raise the clay and shape it.

Naturally, that process applies to an undecorated pot. Very soon you will want to decorate your pots—in that case the decorations, which are done with ordinary paint brushes if of a surface nature (but may be of other forms, such as *sgraffito* or scratchings, achieved with a special instrument), are put on after the pot has been "slipped" but before it is fired.

In an article of this length it is impossible for me to go into more detail, but I have tried to indicate the broad background to pottery, and how to go about learning the craft. There will come the time, however, when you have finished your art school course. Then you may feel the need to have your own potter's wheel and kiln at home, so that you can continue with your hobby (and, incidentally, earn some useful pocket-money if you wish, for there is often a good market for local hand-made pottery).

The cost of installing a good wheel, a reliable small electric kiln, plus materials and tools, etc., could not be much less than £100, and that is a fair sum of money. On the other hand, over a period you could quite easily earn this back by selling some of your produce, even if you confined this to friends. So if you are attracted to the craft of pottery, I do urge you to do all you can, first to learn the craft, and then to carry it on in your own home. It is a hobby which you will find to be a never-ending source of real satisfaction—as well as of extreme practicality. Just think how proud you will feel when your family sit down to a tea-table supplied entirely with your pots!

certain temperature. This is, in effect, a preliminary firing, to make sure the pot is bone-dry before it is glazed.

Glazes are the finishing processes of making a pot—various pigments, oxides, etc., combined with lead and borax, into which the pots are dipped. When the pots are then fired — to temperatures of about 1,100°F.—if making slipware—or much higher, to 1,200–1,300°F., if making stoneware—the glazes form a smooth and watertight covering that is both beautiful and practical.

Here, a worker in a Wedgwood factory is decorating a pot with a paint brush, after the pot has been "slipped" but before it is fired.

ENJOY YOUR OWN MUSIC

Mary Evans

YOUNG MUSICAL STUDENTS, visiting Paris, rarely leave the Capital without seeing the statue of Frederic François Chopin, perhaps the greatest genius of all time in the world of music for the pianoforte.

To pianists, and indeed to musicians generally, Chopin represents much that is worth striving for in music. He wrote solely for the pianoforte and there are few players without some of his works in their repertoire.

At all seasons of the year, Chopin's statue has its visitors, some of them carrying floral tributes, from humble posies of primroses and violets to expensive bouquets. A party of students not long ago placed on the statue a model of a grand piano fashioned entirely in chrysanthemums. It was an exact replica of his piano in his tiny home on the island of Majorca, where he lived for a short time before returning to Paris.

I paused one morning to watch a party of English girls who had made Chopin's statue their rendezvous. One of them, Janine, a descendant of Jane Stirling, Chopin's young Scottish pupil, who befriended him in his last illness, carried a tiny bunch of violets which she placed on the statue.

"Flowers for the Master!" she said. "There is something so friendly and appealing about his music, but I'm afraid I shall never play it as he meant it to be interpreted."

"Why not?" I queried, as I looked at her expressive hands, at the strong, flexible muscles of her tip-tilted fingers which showed the ability to produce exquisite sounds from a beautiful instrument. "Your hands show that you have spent much of your time practising."

Janine confessed that though she spent hours at her piano, she disliked the arduous practice of scales and exercises. "It is such hard and discouraging work and though I have struggled through so many of the difficult studies so essential for successful achievement, I have made very little headway," she said, somewhat disconsolately.

"There is no easy road to success in music," I sympathized. "Achievement lies along the hard road of constant practice. Beethoven, as a student, detested his finger exercises and regarded them as a waste of time, but he was grateful in after life for the 'medicine' of endless finger technique which had been 'prescribed' for him as a boy by his wise instructors."

Janine smiled, but before leaving me to rejoin her companions, told me that though music was her hobby, she had hopes one day of becoming a concert pianist.

Many young musicians have expressed the same wish, but openings are not too frequent. Musicians in the stringed instrument class, such as violinists, cellists, guitarists, and bass fiddle players, are more fortunate, as are instrumentalists in the wood-wind section which comprises the flute, oboe, and the recorder, and in the "brass" section, which covers the trumpet and trombone. Zither players and

Playing a violin with professional confidence.

not be gifted exponents, they learn something of musical appreciation.

School and private amateur orchestras have proved their worth for those wishing to study music as a hobby.

One of the most popular instruments to learn because it takes less time to obtain mastery and requires less practice, is the Recorder, the small reed pipe, capable of producing very sweet tones when played by an expert. It is one of the oldest instruments and its origin goes back to primitive man.

For solo performers, particularly pianists, music as a social asset, is incomparable. Nothing equals the usefulness, or the pleasure that a clever, accomplished pianist can give to a party. The television may break down, or the gramophone records may be forgotten, or lost, but a good pianist is invaluable. She rarely lacks invitations for Christmas parties! Surrounded by her youthful admirers, she is saxophonists are in a class by themselves.

Auditions are held from time to time by application to the Secretary or Director of an orchestra, if music is to be followed professionally, and in each case the musician must be an expert sight reader, able to read and play at once a piece of music without having seen it before. A high standard in the knowledge of harmony and transposition is also essential. Most well-trained musicians are able to transpose music at sight from one key to another.

I advised Janine to seek the counsel of her music teacher before applying for admission to an orchestra.

Most schools nowadays include the theory and practical study of music as part of their educational syllabus. It is an excellent idea and though all students may

A small girl with a large accordion.

Preparing to practise at the piano.

of the rudiments of music is preferable in early childhood. The choice of a suitable teacher should not be undertaken without a good deal of thought. Study at the Royal Academy of Music entails a competitive examination for entrance to the Students' Roll. Beginners are not accepted. The fees are £21 per term. Full details can be obtained from the Secretary. Most towns, however, have a panel of highly qualified music teachers and individual choice is perhaps best in this respect, but it is advisable to choose a teacher who holds the teaching degree as a Licentiate of the Royal Academy of Music.

An alternative to practical musical accomplishment is expression in song. Membership of choirs and amateur operatic societies brings its own reward. Lasting friendships are often made and sometimes lead to the altar! Directors of Education in the various areas, usually have a list of suitable choirs, orchestras, and musical societies.

almost certain of her popularity before she even commences to play.

The Study of the piano accordion also has a large following, but this instrument is heavy and noisy in execution because it dwarfs the sounds of others, though it often gives a romantic background to a picnic!

Popular instruments from a solo point of view, are the violin and 'cello. Like the piano, these require years of practice to obtain expert mastery and control. The delightful rendering of a composition by a brilliant violinist, or 'cellist, well merits the rapturous applause it usually receives.

There are few things in life which compare with the sense of personal satisfaction that comes from the ability to be able to play and interpret expressively the work of a composer, either the Opus of one of the great masters, or something written by a contemporary musician. The applause of an audience, gratifying as it is to the player who has well earned it, rarely takes the place of one's own pride in having given a brilliant performance.

It is never too late to learn, though study

Music is universal and speaks all languages. The English girl on the Continent, though she knows no word of a European

Chopin's piano in the cell of the monastery on the island of Majorca.

language other than her own, is always sure of friendship and hospitality if she is a musician.

There is something enchantingly appealing in the sound of music in the open air, especially in the sunset glow of an evening in midsummer.

The charm of music as its echoes travel across the waters of a river, or a lake, has an indescribably beautiful effect upon the ear of the appreciative listener, particularly if the music is well played and not transmitted through the raucous harshness of a rasping gramophone.

One of the most delightful sounds on the Thames is the "Eton Boating Song", sung in perfect unison by the male voices of practising boat-race crews.

I had rowed from Staines to Windsor and was preparing to tie up my boat to a famous Thames-side landing stage, when I heard the music of a violin and piano playing Kreisler's "Liebeslied". The plaintive, sustained tones of the violin, with its delicate pianoforte accompaniment floating across the water to me seemed all that was necessary to complete a perfect scene.

I looked in the direction of the music which was coming from the open-windowed lounge of a large riverside house. My applause when the music stopped brought two surprised but smiling girls across the lawn to the water's edge.

"That was delightful!" I said. "May I have an encore?"

Janet, the pianist, was the first to reply.

"We are only practising. Our work is not perfect yet and we have much to do before we are ready to play at the Festival."

Please come in and listen," invited Anne, the violinist. "We shall welcome your criticism, for we make many mistakes."

I smiled as I tied up my boat and followed them across the lawn.

"You will not hear any criticism, Anne. I was entranced as I listened to your beautiful playing."

As I neared the house, there were sounds of stringed instruments "tuning up" to a note struck on the piano to bring them up to pitch.

It was my turn to be surprised. There were several girls in the lounge, which had been converted into a large music room. Each girl had an instrument and was sitting in front of a music stand, grouped round an empty chair which did service as a conductor's rostrum.

On the chairs round the walls of the room were a zither, a guitar, a small set of drums and a saxophone.

I felt I had many questions to ask and Janet anticipated my inquiries.

"This is our holiday centre," she explained. "The house has been lent to us by a generous benefactor who has sponsored our musical society. We spend our week-ends here to practise. So far, we are only amateurs, but we hope to become professionals when we have perfected our work."

I felt that it would not be long before they reached this status, as I glanced at the numerous orchestral scores stacked beside the two pianos.

"But how did you all get together? Who taught you? Where have you come from?" I asked.

"We were almost strangers before we got here, though whilst we were studying, we knew that it was our benefactor's wish that a musical society should be formed here and we had to pass rigid tests before we were allowed to become members. We are all winners of musical festivals."

"Where did your members study?" I persisted.

"A few were trained privately, but those who are Londoners, obtained free musical training at school. Every year, the London County Council offers openings for musical scholarships which entitle the successful entrant to four years training. Application for one of the musical scholarships must be made at the age of 12 when the candidate is given a very comprehensive test."

"Is the scholarship student entered for examinations under the Associated Board of the Royal Schools of Music?"

"Yes. It is an understood fact that a scholarship student is expected to take these examinations. She may also, if she wishes, sit for a higher scholarship, say, to Trinity College, or the Royal Schools of Music. There have been a few successes in this respect."

"What happens when you leave school and your free training ends at 16?" I asked.

"Most of us attend the Musical Classes at the London Higher schools such as the Polytechnics. These have classes in the evening for those who are employed in the day time," replied Janet.

"Who plays the zither and the guitar?"

"Those belong to Lina. She bought the guitar for 5s. three years ago, when she was 15, from a school friend, and the zither she brought back from Austria."

Lina demonstrated remarkable skill with both instruments.

"Where did you learn to play?"

"I was given special lessons by a friend," replied Lina "and I completed my training at Evening Classes."

"Our Saxophonist and our drummer were both taught in the same way," added Janet.

"Who taught you the art of the conductor?" I asked Janet, as I gathered that she was the musical director of the orchestra.

"Ah," said Janet smiling. "That is another story. I played the piano in a small orchestra, in Paris, for some time, to gain experience and I was given special lessons in conducting by the director."

"Are lessons given here?"

"Very rarely, especially with the larger instruments. Some of our members have learned to play harmonicas and they have their own band," she added.

Before I left, Janet told me of a school she had opened in London for students of music, singing and dramatic art. She had produced concerts, plays and pantomimes. Her orchestra always accompanied the artists in musical shows. Some of her students were tiny six-year-olds who always gave a good account of themselves at the concerts and proved a popular attraction.

"It is very hard work," said Janet, "but delightful fun."

I promised to attend Janet's next concert and as I released my boat from its mooring post, I heard the stirring strains of Schubert's "March Militaire", played by the orchestra. It followed me for some little distance as I pulled away to my destination on the other side of the river.

PAPER SCULPTURE

Frederick T. Day

THIS IS A SIMPLE YET MOST effective medium through which to work out schemes of decoration, design, patterns, letterings and a modern form of display. Paper sculpture may be applied as a hobby or as a serious craft for such pursuits as window decoration in shop and store, model stage decoration, advertisement layouts, decorations for the club or concert hall and the home.

Diagram 1. The method of paper or card scoring.

Paper sculpture really means the hand modelling of paper or thin card by the means of cutting to shapes, scoring (with the aid of a sharp knife), folding, bending, curling—and creasing—thus producing decorative motifs and designs for border work, paper scrolls, cones, repeat patterns, moulded frame work, lettering, thatching and weaving, to mention a few of the fascinating subjects obtainable through this craft.

THE MATERIALS

Few handicrafts cost less. All that is necessary for serious work is some thick white cartridge paper or thin card obtainable at any stationer's shop or store, some adhesive, a pair of scissors, ruler, pencil, a coil of adhesive tape for joints, a knife or razor blade, a compass and some pins. Oddments of fancy or decorative papers, paper doyleys, serviettes, tinsel and metal papers, lace paper and similar items are most useful in providing frills and fancies to figures—in the form of cuffs, collars, frocks, petticoats, hat trimmings, and so forth, while paper lace will be found ideal for frame work, Valentine cards and their frames, stage model decoration for screens and borders, curtain effects and a host of other detail work to larger pieces.

Gummed paper shapes—stars, circles and other useful shapes—may be obtained ready for use in boxes in the stationer's and will prove an invaluable aid to the handicraft worker. They may be used in decorative work and for articles of dress and facial detail. They save a good deal of extra small cutting. Oval shapes may be used for eyebrows, circles for eyes in figure work, buttons for clothes. Patterned papers will be found most useful in other kinds of decorative schemes and work.

Another aid to paper sculpture is the template or stencil card and in this field there are many ready cut-out stencils which offer the enthusiast and the designer much help in the planning of a piece, motif or design. Few handicrafts require so little material and the necessary paper or card is not really expensive for what it will do. Agile fingers, creative ideas and some imagination will enable the worker to produce some really interesting work. The craft may be continued and taken quite seriously, as many grown-ups are earning their living in working through the medium of paper for window display, advertisement layout and design and so forth. Always consider paper as the medium in this craft and not a substitute for metal, wood or other materials.

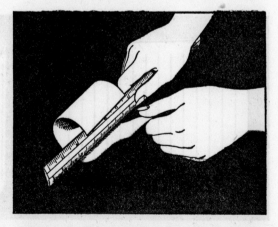

Diagram 2. This shows the angle of pull. Curling paper is an essential operation in paper work.

PRELIMINARY WORK FOR BEGINNERS

Having mentioned the necessary materials and tools for the work, such simple exercises as cutting, scoring, folding, and bending may now follow. Two simple methods which give roundness and solidity to finished work are obtained by folding or bending of paper or card. When bending paper, it must be rolled the long way or grain direction. If it is rolled in the wrong direction, a perfect roll may not be possible, as cracks or breaks may occur—or the paper may fold up in ridges.

The rolled tube or cone is an example of the perfect job and may be the basis for legs, arms, cylinders, tubes, and other components of a piece of work. Paper may be bent to give an arc when desired. Card may be folded to give a definite transition from one level to another and such an angular break may be obtained by scoring.

Paper curling and corrugation are other applications of paper in design. In paper corrugation the paper is merely folded backwards and forwards to give the desired effect. In this way, fans and similar pieces may be obtained.

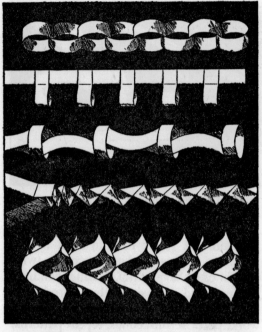

Diagram 4. Some popular forms of decoration with paper are shown above.

Paper or card may be scored with the aid of a knife or razor blade, but the pressure must not be too great as a cut may sever the material. Scoring may be obtained by the use of a blunt instrument, such as a paper knife, and some little prac-

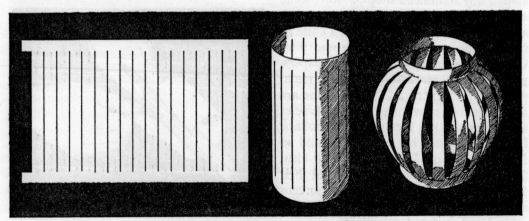

Diagram 3. A rectangle of paper is cut to size and then rolled to make up a cylinder. The cylinder is pressed downwards to form the lantern.

tice will enable the worker to determine the amount of pressure required.

Paper or card curling is obtained by pulling a cut sheet or strip of material under a ruler and, in an upward movement, gently pulling the material away. The paper so treated becomes flexible and may be worked and fashioned as desired.

There is a little more to paper sculpture than these preliminary exercises, but much may be accomplished through these various operations to paper or card. Indication lines or designs may be drawn out first on the paper or card and then neatly cut or scored, folded or bent, corrugated or rolled as desired, to give shape and dimension to the piece of work.

Most paper enthusiasts love to make up sprays and posies of flowers—and here one may press into service paper materials of colour or fancy types, paper lace and so forth. Actual flowers are made up in separate components and assembled and joined together with adhesive: heads, leaves and stems—in three stages. "Master" pieces may be cut from thick card and used as a stencil for repetition work.

Illustration 1 shows the method of paper or card scoring. The neatly drawn line is closely followed with a knife, the cut being just surface made and not too deep to sever the material. Freehand work may follow with practice. First-class let-

Diagram 6. A few simple floral motifs, trees, leaves and flowers.

Diagram 5. An example of thatching and weaving with strips ⅛ in. wide.

tering may be obtained in this way, the individual characters standing out with good effect. While white paper is mostly used, finished work may be hand-tinted in colour, if desired, when the work is completed or placed in position. Good, clean work is essential, so hands should be clean and work cleaned up after the job has been completed. A rubber will be handy for this.

Illustration 2 shows the angle of pull (the angle of pull should be much more acute, but if the picture were correctly illustrated the hand operation would be

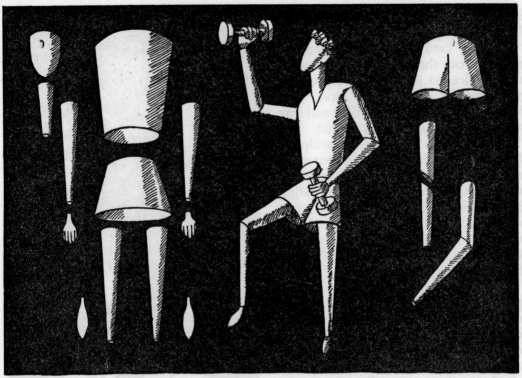

Diagram 7. Cones, tubes and rounded figure work.

practically obscured). Curling paper is an essential operation in paper sculpture and gives the necessary roundness and shape for figure work and cylinders, etc.

Illustration 3 is a display lantern, most effective in both indoor and outdoor schemes of decoration and window display. It is simple yet effective. Here a rectangle of paper is cut to size and afterwards rolled and fixed firmly to make up a cylinder. The cylinder is then pressed downwards to form the lantern, a piece of adhesive tape being used to hold in shape, down the centre.

Illustration 4 shows some popular forms of decoration with paper; the paper used may be coloured or afterwards hand-tinted as desired. Small strips of suitable length are linked up, as shown, and fixed with adhesive to make the chains or loops.

Illustration 5 shows thatching and weaving, which is interesting work and will make up some fascinating patterns, especially where coloured strips are used, for the work. Strips may be $\frac{3}{4}$ inch wide, by any suitable length.

Illustration 6 shows a few simple floral motifs, trees, leaves, and flowers. The design is first drawn out on the cut piece of paper or card—either white or colour being used. The shape is then cut neatly along drawn lines. Creasing and folding takes place to form the shape of the trees and leaves. In the case of the flower, the outside edge of the rolled spiral is pushed down through the centre to form the flower and a clip is needed to hold the shape firmly in position.

Illustration 7 may look somewhat involved, but it really embraces all the exercises mentioned—those of cutting, paper curling (for the hair), paper rolling (for the legs, arms, etc.). Cones and tubes offer endless scope for the more advanced worker.

PICTURE FRAMING AND DECORATION WITH PASSE-PARTOUT BINDINGS

Frederick T. Day

PASSE-PARTOUT BINDING AS A medium for picture, photograph, and drawing framing is practical, inexpensive, and colourful. The selection of a coloured binding for the frame may be chosen to harmonize with existing colour schemes in the home (wall-paper, paint work, etc.). The framed pictures may be varied with any later change in colour scheme or form of decoration. The bindings themselves are made in many bright colours, including gold, silver, wood grains, leather and pebble-finished bindings, so you can see that there is a wide choice of colour. A picture may be framed in one or more colours and many charming frames are obtained from two, or even three, harmonizing colours overlapped, so that just a narrow edge of binding shows along the framed picture.

Individual taste may be freely exercised in style so that not only colour, but shape, type of frame (simple, moulded or deep types) may be produced as desired. Many pictures may be framed from a single coil, and this is certainly a consideration when one considers the cost of metal or wood frames!

It is an ideal means of framing handicraft designs, painted subjects, certificates, sketches, and so on, as it not only preserves the work, but provides the frames for hanging—and for friends to admire. The colour binding chosen should harmonize with the subject, the predominant colours in the picture being the basis of the colour scheme.

Black and white subjects will look best in similar colour bindings, while sepia photographs will look their best in brown or some similar shade. Sea subjects with large areas of sea look at their best framed in blue bindings. If a second colour is used, some thought should be given to the other predominant masses of colour in the picture.

Passe-partout binding is made with a centre crease running the length of the strip, so that a neat and accurate foldline is provided with the binding. Well-moistened tape is essential and this must be firmly pressed home on to the glass and over on to the backing board.

The Simple Frame

The simple frame is very popular for black and white photographs and etchings. The tools required for this style of work are simple.

Some framers' passe-partout—either black, white, grey, or light brown; a pair of scissors and a knife; some glass or glass substitute such as neerglas or micre; some white or grey mounting sheets on which to place the picture into position for mounting; a backing board; some hangers of the adhesive type or pierce-through type should be available.

All these items may be obtained from stationers, stores and many other kinds of handicraft and similar shops. Clothespegs will be found useful to hold glass, backing board and picture together, so that there is no movement while the picture is being framed. A set square is useful in

Diagram 1. Framing the picture in one-colour black pebble binding.

ture. This allows for mitred corners and trimming. Moisten all the strips thoroughly and let the moisture soak into the binding before application.

Illustration 2 illustrates the picture complete with hangers, and pegged to hold into a firm position. The longer edge has been applied to the face of the glass and turned over to the back, ready for pressing down firmly into position.

Illustration 3 shows the mitred corner being cut with the aid of a set square. If you have a steady hand and a good eye, the mitre may be cut with scissors straight away. All four strips are applied in this way and the finished picture is left to dry out before hanging. Any adhesive or finger marks on the glass can be removed with a damp cloth or a little spirit.

If another colour strip is to be applied,

order to help the handicraft worker to produce a good sharp cut for the mitred corners, which are the finishing touches to a good framed subject.

In the case of the simple frame, mount the picture on to a mounting sheet or card —usually white or some suitable toning colour with the picture and cut out some thick cardboard, the same size, for the purpose of a backing board. Glass must be cut to size with the aid of a glass cutter, or glass substitutes may be cut with a pair of scissors. All of these must be exactly the same size. If metal hangers are to be used, these must be pierced through the backing board before the picture is framed—either landscape or postcard—to suit the shape of the picture for subsequent hanging or standing.

Illustration 1 shows a picture of Westminster Abbey being framed in one-colour black pebble binding. All the necessary items are shown, including the pierce-through metal hangers. Here, four pieces of binding are cut about half an inch larger than the edges of the framed pic-

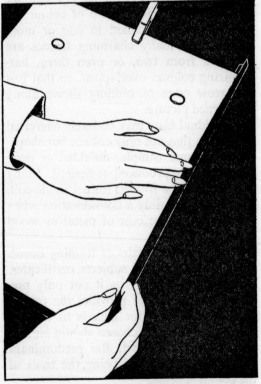

Diagram 2. The application of the first binding strip to glass.

Diagram 3. Obtaining a mitred corner with a set square.

this is cut in the same way, but placed down over the first as an overlap, allowing a narrow edge of the first binding to show.

Illustration 4 shows another picture which has been framed in two-coloured bindings, and, in order to give some depth to the framed subject, the frame has been moulded. This is obtained by cutting strips of card; these are glued along the edges of the glass, thus building up the edge to give depth. The binding is applied to cover this. Any depth frame may be made up by glueing layer upon layer of card to form the mould. The card is also mitre-cornered for effect. The passe-partout binding is applied to cover; two strips, side by side, may be required to cover the extra depth.

Unusual Shaped Picture

While most pictures are square or oblong in shape, there is no reason why many interesting shapes may not be cut out with the aid of a glass cutter. Oval, round, hexagonal, and other shapes are simple to obtain, the binding being pleated for circular shaped frames. Well-moistened strips are essential and this makes the binding very pliable for moulding.

Specimen Cases for Wall Display

Collectors of butterflies, moths, floral items, medals, awards, and so on, may frame them by the passe partout method on the principle of the deep wall frame or show case. Here, the work is similar in all respects, except that thick cardboard is

Diagram 4. A deep-moulded frame, illustrating how this is built up.

shaped panels may be made from these bindings and any colour may, of course, be chosen to harmonize with the colour scheme of the room. Quite plain walls, distemper and paintwork may be relieved with colourful border work neatly planned and carried out in colour. These bindings serve the purpose of wall-paper friezes for borders in many rooms and for a number of purposes. The adhesive is extra strong and adheres to glass and many kinds of difficult surfaces.

Passe-partout may be used to cover plain white wood and cardboard boxes. You can work out many interesting patterns for these. Border work on calendars, binding edges of glass slides, and tea-tray decoration are some of the other items which you will enjoy doing. Black and white bindings laid horizontally and vertically can be used to make a draughtboard pattern and used as a games board. The overlapping and interlacing of bindings can make up many interesting and delightful patterns. Patterns can be worked out on firescreens; the finished effect will not only look very charming but will be practical in the home. This kind of work comes under the heading of passe-partout handicrafts and it has endless possibilities for the girl who enjoys handicrafts.

cut and glued along the edges of the backing board to the required depth. This is then neatly covered with binding and the specimens are then mounted on to the backing board. The glass is fitted on to the four cardboard edges and bound together. These specimen cases are popular in clubs and schools for wall displays.

Wall Panelling and Border Work

Passe-partout binding is made in gold and black and such colours are ideal for wall and panel border work. All kinds of

MAKE YOUR OWN LAMPSHADES

Gwen Rushman

ATTRACTIVE LAMPSHADES CAN make a great difference to the furnishing of a room, but when choosing a style it should be borne in mind for what purpose the room in question is used. A dining-room, study or hall calls for a fairly severe type of shade, while in a bedroom or lounge the frilly or more fancy type of shade can be used.

The wire framework of the shade should

always be covered. This not only improves the appearance of the finished article, but also provides a firm edge to which the actual shade can be stitched. This can be done by winding a matching cotton bias binding round the upper and lower rings and the struts, making sure that the beginning and ending of the binding is secured with a few firm stitches.

Shades can be made in vellum (a firm

oiled paper), buckram (a stiff reinforced cloth) or any firm, fairly translucent paper; also, of course, in material, such as satin, brocade, crêpe—and net or lace over a rayon crêpe foundation. It should be remembered that if the material is too heavy or the colour too dark, then the light will not radiate; the more diaphanous material and pastel colours will produce a better light.

A pleated shade made in a firm translucent paper is simple and very effective, but great care must be taken to ensure that the pleats are exactly even. The length of paper required should be twice the circumference of the lower ring of the frame, and the width of the paper should be the height of the frame, plus 2½ inches to allow the shade to extend beyond the frame top and bottom.

Make marks along the top and bottom of the paper ¾ inches apart and, with these marks as a guide, fold the paper carefully into pleats, fanwise, creasing firmly. Finish with an inside pleat and leave ½ inch for joining (Diagram 1). Punch holes through the front edges of pleats about ¼ inch in from folded edge and 1 inch down from top edge. Make another set of holes through the front edges of pleats, 1½ inches from bottom edge.

Join pleated shade to make a circle and glue the two short sides together. Thread cord through the holes. Place over wire frame and draw up cord so that the shade fits the top and bottom rings of the frame, and fasten off cord securely on the inside of the shade. Arrange the pleats evenly round the frame and secure the shade to the frame, by sewing the cord on the inside of the shade to the lower ring.

A round lampshade can easily be covered in material. A straight piece of material is required, the length being 1½ times the circumference of the lower ring of the frame, and the width of the material being

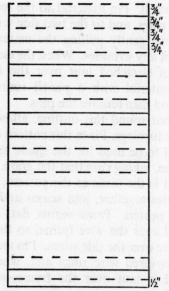

Diagram 1. The hard line denotes fold on righ side, the dotted line denotes fold on inside.

the height of the frame plus 5 inches. Join the two short sides by stitching together ¼ inch from the edge, and then oversew the raw edges to neaten.

On one long side make a hem 1½ inches deep for the bottom of the shade, and on the other long side a hem 1 inch deep for the top of the shade. Run two gathering threads ¼ inch apart on each hem-line. Place wrong side of material over frame and draw up gathers to fit the two rings of the frame. Ease fullness evenly round the frame and stitch on the hem-lines to the upper and lower rings.

To trim a shade for a standard lamp, 1½ yards of 2-inch velvet ribbon is required; for a small shade ⅝ yard of 1-inch ribbon. Cut ribbon in half, tie each piece into a bow and stitch one bow to the top of the shade and the other bow to the bottom of the shade, on the opposite side.

To make a shade for an oval frame, place any odd piece of thin material over one half of the frame, making sure that the true crossway is to the middle of the frame

(Diagram 2). Pin material to the top and bottom rings, and to the two side wires of the frame, gently pulling the material to get rid of any wrinkles. When the material has been stretched taut over the frame, mark material with a pencil round the frame and then remove the pins.

Cut out round this outline, allowing $\frac{1}{4}$ inch for turnings. Place this pattern on the material to be used for the shade and cut out twice, taking care that the grain of the material is the same as the pattern. With right sides together, join seams and oversew to neaten. Press seams flat. Place material over the wire frame, so that the seams are over the side wires. Pin material to the covered wire rings and, when the material is taut over the frame, sew to top and bottom rings. Turn raw edge back on to right side and lightly stitch to wire.

To trim, buy narrow braid for the top of shade and matching fringe for bottom of shade, the length required being the circumference of the shade, plus 1 inch for turnings. Pin braid and fringe over raw edges at top and bottom of shade and sew in position. Half shades for wall brackets can be covered in the same manner.

A small square or round frame, suitable for a hall or landing light, can be covered in 4-ply wool, dish-cloth yarn or string. It is not necessary in this case for the top and bottom rings of the frame to be covered with bias binding, but the wire uprights should be bound with the wool or string, which is being used for the actual shade.

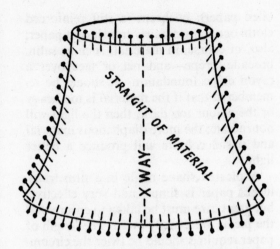

Diagram 2. The material is pinned to frame for pattern.

Wind the wool into a ball. Tie the wool to the bottom ring of the frame and, with the outside of the frame towards you, bring the wool outside the frame and up over the top wire, down inside the frame and under the bottom wire, and then wind once over the bottom ring.

Repeat this process, working round the frame, keeping the strands close together, until the shade is complete. The wool on the top ring should not overlap but lie flat and close together. When joining wool, knot together on the inside of the shade, and fasten off by tying to a strand on the inside of the shade. This shade can be trimmed by oversewing in a contrasting colour on the bottom ring, or by threading ribbon through strands, picking up and leaving 4 strands of the outside wool only.

LEATHER WORK IS FASCINATING

Gwen Rushman

HANDMADE LEATHER GOODS can look most attractive, but it is important to remember that a badly-cut article will never look anything but amateurish, and that the sewing or thonging must be regular and in scale with the article.

There are various types of leather, such

as calf, hide, morocco, skivers, chamois and suède persian, and care should be taken to choose the leather most suitable for each particular piece of work. Calf and hide are expensive so, until you are proficient, it is advisable to chose suède or chamois, or a leather cloth. The latter is not real leather but a manufactured cloth which can be obtained in a number of finishes; it is attractive in appearance and suitable for a beginner to experiment with, as it costs less than leather.

The following tools are "musts" for even the simplest forms of leather work:

1. Ruler, for measuring.
2. Set square, for making accurate corners (preferably one made of transparent celluloid).
3. Knife or razor blade, for cutting straight edges.
4. Scissors, for cutting curved edges.
5. Sixway punch pliers, for punching holes.

It is worth while spending time cutting an accurate paper pattern before actually cutting in leather; for this, stiff brown paper should be used, as this lies flatter on leather than a flimsy paper. Accurate corners are most essential and here the set square should be used. To round a corner, place a coin of suitable size inside the corner and draw round the edge. When placing the pattern on the leather care should be taken to avoid any marks or flaws in the leather.

Diagram 1. Tying corners together.

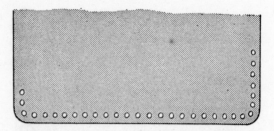

Diagram 2. The corners are rounded and punched.

After carefully marking round the pattern with a sharp pencil, remove the pattern and cut out carefully on the outline. When cutting with a knife or razor blade, the leather should be placed on a hard smooth surface, such as a sheet of zinc or glass, in order to obtain a clean cut.

The leather used for thonging should be strong but thin, so that it is not bulky. Thongs can be purchased ready cut in suède or calf, and these are very suitable for all types of work. The simplest form of thonging is in the form of oversewing. To do this, holes are punched at the edges of the leather and the various pieces are joined together by sewing through these holes with a thong.

To make the holes, hold the sixway punch in the right hand and place the leather between the jaws of the punch, the leather resting on the cutting plate, and press punch together. Give the punch a slight twist before opening the jaws, as this helps the cutting. If the leather is thin, place a postcard underneath to ensure a clean-cut hole. The punch measuring $\frac{1}{8}$ inch or 3/16 inch is suitable for most purposes. The holes should be punched approximately $\frac{1}{8}$ inch from the edge and equally spaced, approximately $\frac{1}{4}$ inch from the centre of one hole to the next.

If two edges are to be thonged together, place the leathers together, punch holes at corners and tie temporarily with cotton (Diagram 1). Then punch holes through both pieces at the same time.

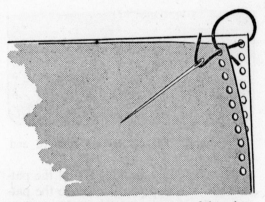

Diagram 3. This shows the starting of thonging.

Generally speaking, corners look much better if they are slightly rounded (Diagram 2); but if a square look is preferred, this can be obtained by cutting the extreme point and working twice into the corner hole.

For easy working, cut the end of the thong to a point and stiffen with a little glue.

To begin thonging two pieces of leather together, pull the thong through the first hole of the top piece only, leaving an end of about $\frac{1}{2}$ inch. Cut this to a point, lay it between the two pieces of leather between the holes and the edge, and fix there with a little glue. Pass the thong into the first hole again, this time from the underside and through both pieces of leather, and then continue through the following holes, as if oversewing. (Diagram 3.)

To fasten off, after thonging through the last hole, pass the thong between the two leathers just below the hole, cut the thong leaving about $\frac{3}{4}$-inch end and glue this on the inside. Alternatively, leave the last few stitches loose, thread the end under them between the two leathers; then draw up the thong tightly and cut off on the inside.

The thonging of a single edge is begun in the same way as for the double edge, the end of the thong being glued on the under side; to fasten off pass the thong back under the last few stitches on the underside, cut off and glue the end.

It is advisable that the first articles attempted should be simple. Then, as experience is gained, something more ambitious can be tackled. Besides handbags, blotters, etc., it should be remembered that slippers can be made in suède, and gloves in chamois or fine leather. Good paper patterns for these can be obtained from art needlework or leathercraft shops and the instructions should be followed carefully to obtain the best results. The following articles are suitable for a beginner, and make useful and attractive gifts.

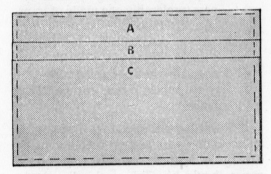

Diagram 4. *Notecase:* Showing C placed on B and C and B placed on A and saddle-stitched together.

Comb Case

Cut two pieces of leather $\frac{3}{8}$ inch wider than the comb and $\frac{1}{4}$ inch longer. At one short end of each piece, cut out a shallow curve approximately 1 inch long and $\frac{1}{4}$ inch deep. Place the two pieces together, with wrong sides facing and curves matching, and punch holes along the other short side and the two long sides. Then thong together.

Notecase

Cut the following pieces of leather :
    A—7 inches by 4 inches.
    B—6$\frac{3}{4}$ inches by 3 inches.
    C—6$\frac{3}{4}$ inches by 2$\frac{1}{2}$ inches.

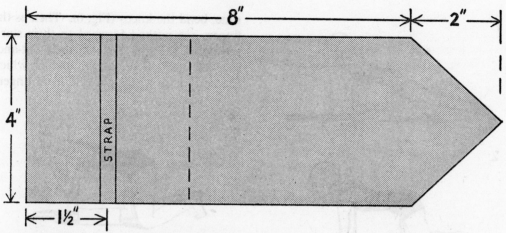

Diagram 5. *Purse:* This shows the strap placed in position. Dotted line indicates fold.

Place wrong side of C on to right side of B, then C and B on to A, the wrong sides of B and A together, so that one long side of each piece is together at base and the short sides match. Stitch together with linen thread, using stab-stitch or saddle-stitch, about ⅛ inch from edge, the stitch being about ⅛ inch long. Fold case in half. (Diagram 4.)

Purse

Make paper pattern as diagram 5 and then cut in leather. Punch holes on short side of purse, and thong. Fold purse up 3½ inches, place strap across front 1½ inches down from thonged edge, and punch holes round all edges but not on fold. Thong all round. The purse can be closed by tucking the flap into the strap.

SWIMMING

Winifred Gibson

PERHAPS YOU WERE YOUNG, only a toddler, when you first learned to swim; perhaps you were older, perhaps (horrible thought!) you may still be a non-swimmer. If so, you can make up for lost time by using the Shallow-water Method, the fastest method of learning in the world today.

Learning is so quick that a film has been made called "From non-swimmer to top board in two and a half hours" and if you do not believe that this is possible, write to The Educational Foundation for Visual Aids, 33, Queen Anne Street, London W.1, who will give you full details of how the film may be hired.

You can learn the land drill if you lie on a biscuit-tin covered by a cushion. Just copy the movements in the following drawings. Figs. 1, 2, 3, and 4 show leg movements. Begin with the legs straight and together. Bend the knees wide but keep the heels touching, then press the soles of the feet outwards until the legs make a wide V and finish with a strong closing of the legs as though they were a pair of scissors.

The arms begin the movement. Press them downwards as they part (Fig. 5). Then drop the elbows and bring the thumbs together below the chin, with palms facing downwards. At the same

time, bend the knees (Fig. 6). Then as the fingers are pushed forward to their starting point, the legs perform their out-and-together movement, at the end of which the body is in a straight line from fingers

Figs. 1, 2, 3 and 4 show leg movements.
Fig. 5. Press arms downwards as they part.

Fig. 6. Bend the knees.
Fig. 7. Stretch body from fingers to toes.
Fig. 8. The shallow-water method.
Fig. 9. Always have a friend standing near.

to toes (Fig. 7). In the water, this position is held while the body glides along the surface as a result of the strong closing of the legs. Breathe out strongly through the mouth as the legs close and during the glide that follows.

The three-foot end of an ordinary swimming-bath can be converted for the Shallow-water Method by sinking a bench into it, the top of which should be an arm's length below the surface. This can be moved to deeper water for people with longer arms (Fig. 8).

Practise your breast stroke until you can glide at least two yards with each stroke and do be sure to learn the breast stroke before you learn the crawl or you may never want to bother to learn the slower stroke. The more strokes you can swim, the less monotonous will be your swimming.

Learning on your back is exceedingly simple if the water is only eighteen inches deep. Lie quite flat, ears below the surface, and relax as you slap your thighs fairly rapidly. In deeper water the chief difficulty is getting on to your feet again and you should always have a friend standing near you (Fig. 9) until you can get up at *every* attempt with absolute certainty. This friend should not touch you until you wish to get up and then she should merely place one hand behind your head and leave the rest to you.

A good way to get up is shown in Figs. 10, 11, 12, and 13. Draw the knees up to the chin after extending the arms sideways along the surface, then nod the head strongly and keep the chin tucked in, as the arms pull deeply through the water. Keep your shoulders under the water until your feet are firmly placed on the bath-bottom and your hands well beyond and in front of you. This is to prevent your over-balancing backwards which is the real danger of a faulty attempt.

10

11

12

13

Figs. 10, 11, 12 and 13 show a good way of getting up on to your feet again.

This is a good time to learn the back crawl. Tackle it before front crawl because breathing presents no difficulty.

Swing the legs easily up and down with the toes turned in. Swing from the hips

Fig. 14. One arm or the other should be pulling the whole time, in the back crawl.

Figs. 15, 16 and 17. Lie face downwards in the front crawl.

and keep the knees loose but do not bend them or let them appear above the water. Only the tips of your toes should appear above the surface and your eyes should look at them without lifting the back of your head above the surface.

At first, use your arms like a pair of oars in a rowing-boat, that is, let both pull together without any pause. When you can pull strongly, work them alternately and keep them moving. One arm or the other should be pulling the whole time. There is no pause (Fig. 14). You will learn to relax as you swim longer and longer distances. If you stick to this stroke until you can swim one hundred yards really well, you will learn the front crawl much more easily and quickly.

The principle of the front crawl is the same as that of the back crawl. You lie face downwards, of course, but the leg stroke is the same. The arm action is performed alternately but the pull is deeper, because you are in a better position to drive the arms deeper. For this reason, front crawl will always be a faster stroke than back crawl. The arms can move together during first practices (Figs. 15, 16, 17, 18, 19, and 20).

It is the breathing that presents difficulty when face downwards but if you remember to turn your head to its natural side just after the hand behind your head has got ready to press downwards on the water, you will find that air can be taken in quite easily provided you expelled

Figs. 18, 19 and 20. The arms can move together during the first practices for the front crawl.

air strongly into the water before turning the head.

DIVING

Do not wait until you feel you are a competent swimmer, before beginning to learn to dive. There is a good deal you can learn about diving without going into deep water.

Breath control is most important and you can practise this in a standing position. Hold the bath rail, fill up with air and put your head under the water. Try to keep it there until you can count twenty quite slowly. Then open your eyes and for ever afterwards keep them open whether your head is below the water or not. Many learners keep their eyes tightly shut most of the time. This is a sign that their muscles are not relaxing, which is why they quickly become fatigued.

Divers enter the water head down, legs up. You can get used to this position by performing a handstand in three feet of water. Practise until you can balance your body in an upright position, while you again count twenty and hold your breath.

You might then go into about five feet of water and try a seal dive.

Keep your hands by your sides as you let your body sink into a handstand position. You will not bump your head in five feet of water. It goes down quite gently. Lie on a folded towel which should overhang the bath edge to protect your shins, until you are expert enough to make a vertical entry.

To avoid flat diving, learn to somersault first. Grip the edge of the bath with your toes, legs wide apart, grasp your ankles and merely overbalance on to your shoulder-blades. Put your feet together for the next somersault and grasp the backs of the knees. Give a slight push with the feet and let your rounded shoulders meet the water. Too big a push may cause the water to slap you lower down your back. We usually get slapped

for the mistakes we make in diving, but if we learn the somersault way those slaps don't hit us in the face.

To progress from the somersault to the dive, stand in diving-flight position, push upwards and go over as for a somersault. Keep at this exercise until your entry is clean and vertical. For this, the water should be not less than seven feet six inches deep, and a foot deeper for fully grown people.

The arm-swing need not be learned until last. With arms raised forward to shoulder height and shoulder-width apart, they are dropped to the sides and then swung forward and upward to flight position. The spring, that is, the push-upwards of the feet, occurs just as the hands reach eye-level in their upward swing. The body remains straight from fingers to toes during the whole of the flight (Dia. 25), and the entry into the water should be as nearly vertical as possible. See Figs. 21, 22, 23, and 24.

The best way to improve your swimming is to work for the graded examinations of the Royal Life Saving Society. You never know when such qualifications may be useful to you.

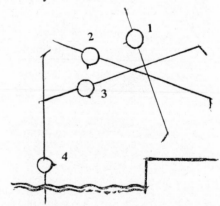

Figs. 21, 22, 23, 24 and Diagram 25; 1, 2, 3 and 4 illustrate diving-flight positions.

BALLET DANCING

Peter Craig-Raymond

BALLET AS A HOBBY HAS ONE advantage, almost peculiarly its own. Even if you never set foot on the stage your training as a dancer will be useful to you.

I had this borne in on me some years ago when, attending (very reluctantly) a county ball in the wilds of north Scotland, my host beamed as his daughter walked into the room. "Know why I'm proud of her?" he asked me. "Well, she's attractive, well-dressed and amazingly confident for a fourteen-year-old," I answered.

"You've hit it"—he growled, not too pleased that I had not let him tell me the answer—"she's as poised and sure as her mother, more than twice her age. Know why?" I could have told him again, but politely I let him tell me this time: "Ballet, that's what. Can't see anything in it myself, but it certainly gives 'em poise."

That was too limited a view.

Ballet training, by strengthening various uprighting muscles and stressing bodily posture, can be as important to the girl who will never dance as to the dancer. Socially, that is. The whole technique of ballet training, except the "turned out" figure it demands, produces a confident, sure, poised figure which is the ideal for any girl.

I think most parents today realize that the younger this poise can be ingrained in the child, the better. One of the ordeals of growing up is "facing a room" or meeting new people at any time. Ballet training dispels this embarrassment by making the girl so sure of herself, physically, that meeting a crowd becomes an easy and sociable event, as it should be. I think that most of us, boys as much as girls, would have gone gratefully to ballet, if it had then been as available as it is today.

This is the social side of what can be hobby or career—and is often both.

Another side of ballet as a hobby is the sheerly physical one. Working under a dance teacher you will be under constant pressure to think of your body . . . not as a thing that you feed, sleep, and use to move with . . . but as an important part of you which, to have its best effect, must be kept continually in good physical shape. Here the ballet exercises come in, but, still more important, this unceasing supervision from your teacher which says: keep fit. It is becoming gradually realized that ballet tuition is better for your bodily health than conventional gymnastic training.

It's worth remembering here that no amount of dress sense, fashion flair, cosmetic knowledge or the deeper feminine instincts will successfully help you over the flaw of having an uncontrolled body. Nobody need have. The body responds to training and sharp, inner discipline as readily (more readily, perhaps) than the mind. And it never hurts.

Of the tens of thousands of girls in Britain who take ballet training, not very many make a professional career of it. But even fewer ever regret the hard training they have undergone. No woman will ever regret her physical fitness or her good control over her body's movement.

Another side of ballet as a hobby is the friendship it can bring. Not just the friends

Practising at the barre during ballet rehearsals.

who come to tea, but a collection of young people all interested in *ideas*. In this atmosphere, which can mix happily with your working life, you can keep abreast of current thinking and achievements in the theatre and arts and in general affairs. The typist who never thinks away from her machine and the occasional novel is not the product of a ballet training.

Just as dance training makes your body

a hair-trigger instrument ready to jump at a signal, so the same training makes your mind an open, idea-thirsty thing. Why is this? Simply because all things function better under the stress of hard work. This sounds, perhaps, like the old-time church minister or teacher... but there he had something. The more fit you are for work, the more fit you are for play, too.

Ballet makes you work, it opens up your body, tires it, forces it to rest and regenerate itself. And, on your mind, it has much the same effect. Altogether you live better if you work under a dance teacher—or under various other teachers.

Taking it that you are not to be a professional ballet dancer, where does your hobby lead you?

First, and all important, it works for your benefit as I have already described. After that it can work in many ways. You

Margot Fonteyn and Michael Somes in a scene from "Swanlake."

will, no doubt, take part in annual recitals at your local ballet school. These, produced by your teacher, prove the usefulness of co-operation and also help you appreciate professional ballet. You may also appear in charity shows and in local pantomimes.

Above all, this ballet training you take will give you a fresh, keen interest in the world outside of your own home and hometown. It stretches the seams of your mind, gives a heave to sluggish imaginations, and gives you a social and conversational interest which develops over the years.

This early training of yours will have its effect when, sitting in the theatre, you know something of what is going on. When you watch films with dance elements, when you read any of the very large number of books on the dance now being written. And ballet books cover a wide field, inside their own limits. Text-books, biographies, argumentative essays, diaries, photographic records... all can be found with ballet as their starting-point.

There are many other valuable pointers one could make concerning ballet. The respect it gives you for your partners, for

Daphne Dale—one of Britain's youngest and most successful ballet dancers.

one. In ballet the boy must respect his partner, and the girl be worthy of it.

In a London theatre, just a few evenings before I sat down to write this, I was introduced to the Yugoslavian dancer Milorad Miskovitch. At this time, as you may remember, he was dancing with Alicia Markova as she appeared in Manchester, Glasgow, Leeds, Bristol, Southampton, and other towns. I told him that, as the third or fourth partner of this great ballerina, he was in an incredibly fortunate position to further his own work.

He agreed, and went on to detail some of the things which dancing with Markova had given him.

I was struck by one point he stressed: "She makes me feel so definitely her cavalier—nothing is too good for her."

And that is what I meant by respect. If it can have its effect on a dancer of Miskovitch's ability, it certainly is felt by all the thousands of young people who learn ballet. If ballet training had no other end, this "respect for each other" which it engenders would make it worthwhile today.

Happily, and I hope I have made the point here, ballet training has many other facets which make it an excellent choice as a hobby—and, maybe later, as a career.

But, either way, I have a clear mind about suggesting it to you or, as the case may be, adding my voice to other persuasions.

I have heard many people often complain of ballet's demands—but I have never met anyone who died of them.

TAP DANCING FOR RECREATION

Zelia Raye

MANY PEOPLE THINK OF TAP dancing as something to be watched rather than experienced, but its fascination has sent many a youngster to the dance studio. The film and stage have set a high standard for the professional dancer, but it is the amateur, who loves it as a form of dance, who will discover what it has to offer as recreation.

If a subject is to be taught correctly, the method should have the same basic fundamentals whether for amateur or professional use. The tap terminology which was created by me for the stage branch of the

Imperial Society of Teachers of Dancing Inc., is a basis for tap technique and, of course, should be mastered. However, it is the creative approach which should be considered more progressive than the imitative, although learning good dances is part of training and gives encouragement for further development. The danger lies in learning too many steps without understanding the other qualities that make a good tap dancer. Many over-ambitious dancers attempt difficult steps too soon and execute them at too fast a tempo, overlooking the fact that clear taps are an essential. They thus retard their own progress by ignoring tone and quality. How much more satisfying it is to concentrate on simple steps and develop a good feeling for time, rhythm and musical phrasing. As one progresses, more attention should be paid to posture and gesture. It is the com-

bination of steps together with the above qualities which make a good tap dancer as against the ordinary "hoofer". These qualities add style and grace to the dancer, but it is the spirit of dance that makes it alive and vital.

Many students who enter for our Tap Medal tests are nervous. They lack confidence and therefore do not dance with spontaneity. They should realize that if they do not enjoy dancing, neither can the onlooker. Much could be done to improve this state of affairs by forming practice groups, the members having fun and gaining confidence by practising together.

Now we come to the question of creating. With the introduction of syncopation and interesting rhythms in modern music, the scope for original composition is enlarged. With a limited amount of technique a very interesting group composition can be created, but, however simple the steps, it is important that the individual should make a special effort to get them as near perfect as possible so that the unity and harmony of the group should function at as high a level as possible. All this should be exciting and beneficial, both mentally and physically. Members should experiment by creating a modern folk dance in the tap idiom. It should be like a game set to music and nothing fosters enjoyment like a game. The choice of good music is important. Stimulating music has the effect of improving the execution of a very simple step. The work should always be kept within the capabilities of the group, preferably a mixed group. This suggestion of forming groups is not intended to take the place of dance schools, where tuition is obtained from capable teachers. The object of the group would be purely recreational and would naturally depend on good leadership. It would bring tap dancers together, help them to brush up what they have learnt in the schools and develop those additional qualities previously mentioned.

I write this article hoping it will stimulate interest in a form of dance that lends itself to infinite possibilities for enjoyment and recreation if the spirit of co-operation is there.

Those of you who have never attempted a tap step, may I persuade you to "have a go"? When you hear a good tune, do you unconsciously tap your foot in time with the music? That is quite a good start and shows that you have rhythm latent in you. Now sit on a chair with knees slightly apart, feet parallel and flat on the ground and under the knees.

(1) Lift your right foot and press ball of foot on the ground. Notice that the heel is raised off the ground.
(2) Lift left heel off the ground and execute a heel beat. Rather as you would do, if cracking a nut.
(3) Execute a heel beat with right heel.

Keep saying, "Ball, heel, heel – right, left, right".

Repeat, commencing with left foot – left, right, left.

Now count, 1 & 2 3 & 4.

When you feel confident, stand up and try this step to a slow foxtrot. You can probably do this in a few minutes, and if so, my advice is to carry on and learn tap dancing. You will soon find that you are educating your feet and if you keep telling them what to do, it is surprising how soon they will respond.

To continue, here is a test for the more ambitious. As I wish to emphasize the importance of rhythm, I am limiting the tap technique to ball and heel beats.

Rhythm 8 & 1 2 & 3 & 4 5 & 6 & 7
. . . .

Notice that the count of *6* is a missed beat, otherwise the rhythm is even.

First count and clap your hands to this rhythm until you feel it.

. 8	Step on ball of right foot
. &	Heel beat left
. 1	Heel beat right
. 2	Step on ball of left foot
. &	Heel beat right
. 3	Heel beat left
. & 4	Spring backwards on right and left foot
. 5 &	Step on ball of right foot and heel beat on right
. 6	Miss beat
. & 7	Step on ball of left foot and heel beat on left

The following rhythm step is most useful, as it can be done in a variety of ways, making interesting patterns, – Forwards, backwards, sideways, and turning. It is also a good rhythm for a group forming a circle or danced with a partner.

– 1 **2**	Step forward right
. 3	Close left to right foot
– 4 **5**	Step forward right
. 6	Close left to right
– 7 **8**	Step forward right

The counts of *2, 5* and *8* are missed beats.

Repeat, commencing with the left foot.

Rhythm & 1 2 & 3 & 4 & 5 & 6 & 7
. . . .

& 1	Stamp right stamp left
2	Heel beat left
& 3	Brush back left & step on right ball of foot (heel off ground)
&	Heel beat left
4	Heel beat right turning left toe up
&	Pick up left foot (sharply slap ball of foot backwards removing heel of same foot)
5	Heel beat right
&	Step backwards on left turning right toe up
6	Pick up right
&	Heel beat left
7	Toe tap right to left diagonal back

Do your best with this—improvize to foxtrot and tango music and have lots of fun.

GUMMED STRIP MOULDING AND MODELLING

Frederick T. Day

HERE IS A COMPARATIVELY new handicraft for all ages which is becoming increasingly popular in many ways. Gummed-strip, the continuous strip of brown and coloured gummed tape has been used for many years for repairing torn and broken books, temporary repairs to many household articles and for packing parcels. This material has gained new appeal in the field of moulding shapes from formers or basic moulds on to which the tape is wound, thus taking the shape of the mould itself. In this way, many articles, models, toys and useful objects may be produced from tape, not the least, a first-class dressmaker's mould, which may be produced by winding moistened tape round the body.

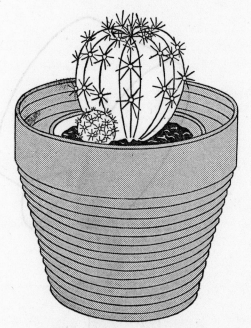

Fig. 1. Bowl or vase for plants.

Gummed strip has many other applications and being available in strip form and in many colours (about one inch wide) first-class lettering, notices, and showcards, border work, binding and similar work may be carried out for the club or wherever such things are required. The handicraft is inexpensive, a coil of some 120 feet costing about one shilling.

MOULDING FROM COILS

Among the many articles which may be produced from moulded shape with gummed strip are flower-pot stands or display stands, lens hood for the camera, brush or pen-end protector and many other objects. In every case, some tools are necessary, but only simple items generally available in the home.

As gummed strip will stick to surfaces when moistened, the shape from which the article is obtained must be covered with tissue paper, muslin, or scrim, or in some cases, dusted with French chalk. A pair of scissors will be needed, and a razor blade or sharp knife to cut the moulded tape from the mould or shape. A damper is also very useful if much sticking is involved as the tongue, while being the most natural damper there is, should not be used for the longer jobs. A damp cloth or brush moistener is best and the gummed strip should be thoroughly moistened before application. Moulded shapes are obtained by applying layer upon layer of well-moistened tape on one another. When dried out, the tape thus applied becomes a hard and strong moulded shape which may be handled and the mould itself is quite waterproof.

Such items as balloons when inflated make first-class shapes from which to mould other shapes. Plasticine, wax, clay, plaster of Paris, and so forth, when moulded to shape may be used to build up a gummed strip model, many copies being made where repetition work is needed. In this case, the applied tape is neatly cut away from the mould by the means of a cut line with a sharp knife. As the initial shape has been protected as described with paper or some other means, no tape will adhere. The balloon or similar inflated object used is merely deflated and withdrawn after the tape has been cut.

The tape may be applied to any thickness desired for strength and long durability. Where finished work has to be immersed in water, as in the flower vases and pots and so forth, the finished work is treated by painting or varnishing in order to provide a waterproof surface to resist water penetration. Moulded work may therefore be used for flower vases and pots. Such work may be treated with a transfer design or painted with a motif for added attraction before varnishing.

Gummed strip made up in tube form has many novel and interesting uses. Legs

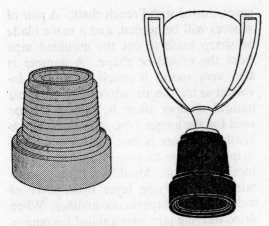

Fig. 2. A trophy or cup display stand.

for puppets, model work and tubes may be made in any diameter so that body, arms and legs may be prepared and assembled. New models may be made up by using old models or toys as a basis upon which to work.

Bowl or Vase for Plants or Flowers

This simple yet effective model will enable the newcomer to the handicraft to get the "feel" of the material and the general idea of the work. A flower-pot may be used for this but it must first be covered with plain paper as described, to prevent moistened tape from adhesion. Several rounds of wet tape are neatly applied or stepped up as shown and a circular piece of cardboard is cut out for the base. This is fitted into position and stuck into the base. The flower-pot is finally removed, leaving behind a moulded shape which may be decorated as desired. It must be varnished for outdoor use or where water is involved.

In addition to using a mould for such work, the tape itself may be wound in a suitable ring and then pushed into shape in order to produce a pot shape. The telescopic possibilities of tape are such that many tubes, cones and other shapes may

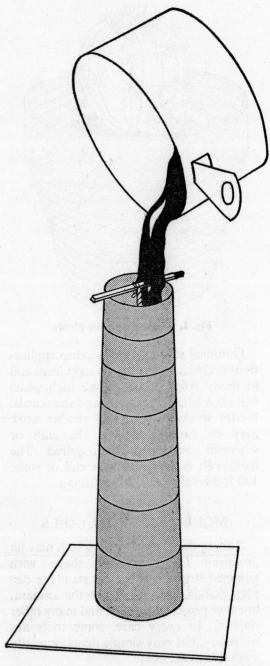

Fig. 3. How to obtain decorative and coloured candles from ordinary white wax tape is shown above. White wax is melted down and some suitable colouring matter added.

be obtained by winding off some tape from a coil in suitable quantity to produce such work. Interesting bowls and other shapes are obtained this way (Illustration 1).

Illustration 2 shows a similar piece of work—a trophy or cup display stand—which may be produced in much the same way from wound gummed strip. Here, the work is tiered for effect. A cut circle of card is fitted into position to complete the stand. This may be obtained by using another cut stand as a basic mould or by wound tape pushed or "telescoped" into shape. Neatly wound tape gives a good final finish and this may be painted black as desired.

Decorative Wax Candles

In Illustration 3 the method of obtaining decorative and coloured candles from ordinary white wax tape is shown. The white wax is melted down and to this is added some suitable colouring matter. Odds and ends of lipstick cases provide a good colouring material. A wound tube

of tape is made up similar to that shown and the wick obtained from the candle is suspended across and down the centre with a nail. The coloured melted wax is then poured into the shape and left to harden. The tape mould is cut away, leaving behind a moulded candle in colour, complete with wick. Corrugated paper may be used inside the gummed strip and this will give a good effect to the final decorative candle. Coloured candles may be made for a small fraction of the cost of a coloured one and then there is the fun in creating one's own colour and styles.

Lens Hood and Filter Holder for Camera

This useful item is shown in Illustration 4 and it is very simple in construction. The amateur photographer will appreciate the use of the filter holder and will know something of the cost of these objects—something in the region of 7s 6d. each! Only a small quantity of gummed strip is needed and the lens hood is made up on the same principle as the trophy stand.

Fig. 4. A lens Hood and Filter Holder for the amateur photographer.

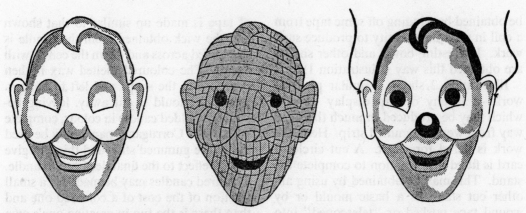

Fig. 5. Masks and Heads suitable for carnivals and plays.

Moistened gummed strip is wound to the shape as shown in our picture, taking good care of diameter for accurate fitting. The circular filter piece is added at the completion of the job while the lens hood may be suitably painted with black or silver paint or a strip of silver paper may be applied to cover, thus giving the appearance of a metal fitment. Passe partout binding may be used for this finished effect. After some experience with this handicraft, coils and cones may be wound without the aid of a former or mould.

Masks and Heads—Puppetry

The possibilities of this craft in connection with the making-up of masks and heads for parties and other special occasions and for puppetry will soon be realized. Puppets may be made from moulded shapes together with tubes, of suitable diameters for the legs and arms, etc.

Illustration 5 shows masks and heads suitable for carnivals, plays, stage work, parties and other festive occasions. They may be made up in any size from the initial mould used for the work. Clay, plasticine and so forth may be used as a base for the mould and the finished detail added to the moulded shape obtained in this way. Funny, serious or well-defined

effects may be obtained as desired. The basic mould must be protected in order to prevent tape adhesion in the usual way. Any number of masks may be obtained from the initial mould, but the facial treatment afterwards may be varied if necessary. Any additional fittings such as ears, etc., may be fitted afterwards.

Dressing your own Doll

In Illustration 6 the method of obtaining a doll model from an existing toy is shown. This work can lead on to the more serious dressmaker's mould used for the purpose of making up dresses, costumes, etc., and indeed, many professional tailors make up dressmaker's dummies or moulds with gummed tape from the actual figure.

First, let us deal with the work of obtaining a doll. Any doll may be used on which to build up a doll model and this may be dressed as desired afterwards. First cover the model with muslin or thick paper and wind well-moistened gummed strip round the body, as illustrated. When completed cut neatly down the centre and then join the cut thus made with tape. The legs and arms in this case are, of course, treated likewise and the finished parts joined up.

Teenagers and others may make up professional tailors' dummies in much the same

GUMMED STRIP MOULDING AND MODELLING

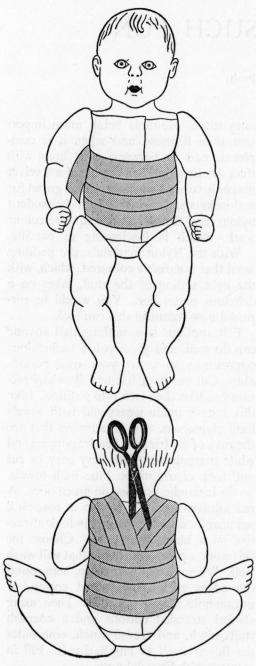

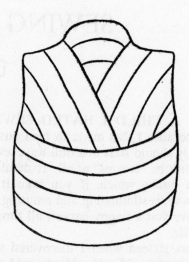

Fig. 6. How to obtain a doll model from an existing toy is shown above and on right.

way. Gummed strips will help the dressmaker by providing a really true and accurate figure dummy of the body.

First, a fine muslin is used over the body as the basis on which to build up the shape. An old bathing-costume may be worn but whatever is used, it must cover the shoulders. Start to wind (and here, some help must be obtained) well-moistened tape round the figure from the waist upwards. These are applied to the muslin cover over the body. Smooth the tape well to the figure to avoid unevenness and a final good finish. As soon as the mould has been formed it is removed from the body by cutting up the back and afterwards neatly joined together again. Further layers of gummed strip are applied in order to give a firm casing and strength. The final and finished replica is covered with jersey stockinette and the whole is then mounted on an adjustable stand. A coat hanger and centre pole may be used as a support, together with a floor stand or legs. Accurate dresses may now be made, giving a correct fitting to the figure.

These are just a few of the many fascinating models which may be made up with gummed strip in the new handicraft.

SEWING IS SUCH FUN

Ursula Bloom

AS A CHILD I HATED SEWING because I was made to hem dusters. Nobody should start in a dull way; sewing shouldn't be "lessons" at all. It should be fun, a hobby which, if you take it the right way, is stimulating and amusing and will give you a happy harvest all through your life.

I was sixteen when I discovered what an exciting world embroidery could open for me. I made fascinating gifts for others, lovely lingerie for myself, and a bottom drawer that everyone envied.

It is important to start on this sort of venture by doing something you will really like, and which is fairly certain of success. For that reason I would suggest quilting. You buy a traced muslin pattern, which you tack to the back of your material. Run along this pattern with a regular run-

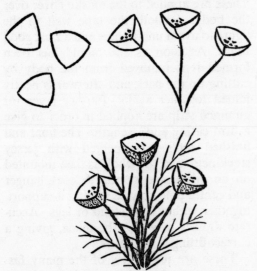

Felt Poppies are tacked into place. Add surround in shaded green.

ning stitch, evenness being more important than fineness, and when it is completed, pad in between your lines with thick Berlin wool used double. Fine velvet makes luxurious cushions; silk is grand for bed jackets and sachets, whilst the modern nylons lend themselves to exquisite colour work, which is fascinating to execute.

With the Nylon materials, use padding wool that is garishly coloured, which, with the light veiling of the stuff, takes on a delicious pastel hue. You would be surprised how beautiful this can look.

Felt appliqué is something that anyone can do well, and gives you a tremendous opportunity to assert your own personality. Cut out your felt to follow any picture you like, then tack into position. Like this I have made weary old bath towels look glamorous, and face towels that are the envy of my friends. Scarlet poppies and white marguerites (both very easy to cut out) look charming on blue bath towels. So do Icelandic poppies on green ones. A red lobster, a crab, a couple of rose-pink sea anemones and a sea urchin look attractive on a black bath towel. Choose for this work a good-quality felt that will wash well. When tacked into place, hem round the edges with self-coloured cotton, or button-hole if you prefer it. Then using shaded stranded cottons and a coarsish stalk stitch, and crewel stitch, embroider the flower itself to emphasize it. Fill in stamens with French knots.

I first got this idea when I wanted table napkins to match a dinner service which had the famous Napoleonic ivy leaf pattern on it. I found that from the garden

An example of a gaily coloured tapestry covering for a stool.

ivy, I could cut out dozens of green felt leaves, then hem into place. With a lighter shade I marked in the veinings, then joined in with the stalks. It was a quick job, and very, very effective.

Growing more enthusiastic, I enlarged the idea, and made Hungarian ladies with wide embroidered skirts in gay colours; they looked most realistic when finished. There is really no end to what can be done.

The other day I was talking to quite a little girl, and I showed her how to cut out angel fish in felt, and how to embroider after with black. As you grow more experienced, you go farther, but you will be surprised to find how easily it comes to you, and how very interesting it is.

In crewel stitch you can embroider almost anything you fancy. I have always found that it added enormously to a design to give it the original touch by adding a tiny motto, something gaily light-hearted, which makes it truly different. Your birth flower is a thought, your sign of the zodiac, something which really gives it part of your personality.

Don't fall into the mistake of too much embroidery only in outline. People do this because it appears to take less time, but you can never hope to get the same effect this way. If you shrink from the thought of all the filling-in, use a backing of appliquéd linen which will form its own background in colour, and then work on top of it in a fairly thick outline. Coloured linen hankies are useful, because you can be sure that they are colour proof, and will not run, but be sure to choose the firmer kind of linen, otherwise they have a tendency to fray.

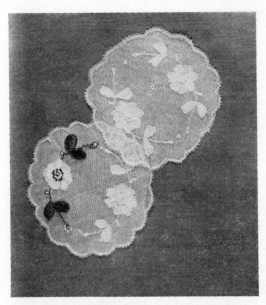

Mats for a dinner table can be embroidered with flowers and leaves.

Embroider butterflies—wild birds—fungi. Anything that you personally find enthralling, because *the things that you like best, you do best!*

A charming form of work, if you are not very sure of yourself, is to tack a canvas over your material, and do cross stitch embroidery through this, pulling each stitch very tightly. When done, draw the canvas threads gently away, one by one. You have to be sure that nowhere you have stitched through the canvas itself, else, of course, you cannot move it. Use bright, gay colours—the sort they employ a great deal in the Balkans—emerald green, ruby red, and royal blue. With this idea, you can add motifs to your hankies, embroidered ends to your scarves, and do all manner of things.

If you only choose to use your needle as an artist uses his pencil, then you will find this the happiest hobby of all. Always make something that is different and which expresses yourself rather than copies other people, for this gives a wonderful feeling of self-confidence, and you will, in the end,

do work that will make you very, very proud.

Think for yourself, and work it out with your needle.

My mother always said to my brother, "When you marry, choose a girl who can sew, because she will be a happy girl!" and I believe she was quite right. Think of what I have said, because I am quite convinced that there is a tremendous lot of happiness tucked into a needle, and it is a joy that will last you for all your life.

This pretty little felt picture would make a charming addition to a nursery. You need an oblong piece of felt, 13″ by 10″ for the background, a few scraps of different greens for the hillocks, black for shoes and hair, white for bonnet, blouse and socks, cherry red for the dress and flesh colour for legs, arms and face. The daisy chain and the daisies on the grass are embroidered in white and green, and the clouds and birds in white. Brer Rabbit is added in brown chain stitch. If you are going to frame and cover the picture with glass the pieces need only be stuck on. Otherwise they are stitched with matching cotton. The whole can be pressed on the wrong side over a damp cloth, when finished.

CANOEING

Sylvia Gregg

CANOEING IS A PARTICULARLY suitable sport for girls because, to excel at it, needs skill rather than strength. This was proved by two Deal schoolgirls who took up canoeing at their youth club, and a few months later paddled across the Channel to within a mile of the French coast. Newspaper reporters who met the girls on their return were amazed to see two average fifteen-year-olds instead of the Amazons they had expected.

Another point about canoeing is that it provides all the excitement of a thrilling sport with the satisfaction of a useful hobby. For, apart from the various forms of canoe racing, canoeing is a means of spending a cheap holiday or taking a healthy, but not too energetic day out.

It was a Scotsman, John MacGregor, who started canoeing as a sport, way back in 1865. He was a great traveller and all-round sportsman, and after he had injured a leg in an accident, he designed a small boat, easy to handle, that enabled him to carry on with the open-air life he loved. The boat followed the lines of the Eskimo kayaks he had seen north of the Arctic Circle, and caused quite a sensation as he travelled the rivers of Britain and Europe.

However, it is only since the war that canoeing has become really popular. New clubs have been founded all over Britain with members who are most of them young, and always keen.

The first step for a beginner is to be able to swim, for the best canoeists capsize sometime or other. The next, is to buy a good second-hand folding boat. (A folding boat is light enough to carry and can be taken on the railways free of charge.) If possible, get an experienced canoeist to examine the boat for wear, and always try out the boat on water before buying.

A kayak-type boat costs from fifteen to twenty pounds second-hand. There are build-it-yourself canoe-kits consisting of frame, rubber skin, canvas deck, double-bladed paddle, etc., for about twelve pounds, and if you have a handy brother, the job could well be done for five pounds or less.

It is a good idea to join a local canoe club or to take a training holiday at one of the Central Council of Physical Recreation centres. This way you will be helped to develop a style which will bring the most results for the least effort. And this is the art and ease of canoeing—a rhythmical stroke which carries one over the water without being sore or sorry for it the following day.

The other type of canoe is the Canadian —an open, hollowed-out craft with which a single-bladed paddle is used. It is very similar to the boats one sees Red Indians using in illustrated history books. The Canadian type canoe is a very hardy craft which can be poled like a punt. Two people can sleep in it and the canoes are often tastefully furnished with carpets and cushions! But the Canadian is more expensive than the kayak and more difficult to transport.

Racing requires a different technique from that used by the cruising canoeist. Racing craft are so finely balanced that it takes some practice to learn how to sit in one. But, within a year it is possible to be up to standard for entering national championships and not do too badly in them, either.

There are three main classes for racing—Canadian, kayak, and slalom. This last is a thrilling sort of obstacle race in rough water (sometimes called "white" water). Hidden rocks, whirlpools, weirs, and stakes specially planted for the race, have to be negotiated quickly and without touching the obstacles. Slalom needs a great deal of experience behind one.

But MacGregor designed his boat for cruising, and the 2,000 miles of waterways in Britain provide ample opportunity for this. The Thames from Lechlade to Richmond ripples and rushes past beautiful scenery—Oxford, from the river, for in-stance, is one of *the* sights of Britain. And in every part of the country are quiet back-waters or mountain streams that have just as much attraction for canoeists as our better-known rivers.

A few last tips—take a pride in your canoe and keep an eye open for wear and tear. A patch in time has saved many a damp walk home. If you're on a week-end cruise travel light but sensibly. Even in the Devizes to Westminster race (the course, over 100 miles long, is covered in about 24 hours), one of the toughest canoe races in the world, competitors have to carry a change of clothing, cooking and camping equipment, and, of course, food and water, although they wouldn't dream of making use of any of it while they were still in the race.

And if you *do* capsize, and help is avail-

Canoeists believe in waterproofing themselves before setting out.

Pupils of the South Oxford Senior Secondary School, in canoes they have built themselves, show how these craft should be handled.

able, don't try to swim for it but hang on until you are fished out. On the other hand, if you are there when someone else falls into the water, always rescue the canoeist first, and the canoe later.

If you want information about canoe clubs and canoeing waters in Great Britain, write to Mr. John Dudderide who is the Secretary of the British Canoe Union, at The Briars, 33 The Avenue, Radlett, Herts. You will find him most helpful. Happy canoeing to you all!

CLIMBING

Odette Tchernine

ALTHOUGH ALL - THE - YEAR - round playtime is fun, the holiday fun is the most anticipated. You plan for it a long way ahead, which is often just as good as the real thing. Then there's the thrill of setting off in coach, train, boat, or even 'plane for new experience and adventure. It may be you will stay at a pony-club camp to learn about riding, and the care of horses. Again you may visit a tiny fishing village with great rocky cliffs, or you and the family, or you and a party of friends, might take a trip over the hills and far away.

You will want to explore around cliffs and take walks over rolling downs or moorland.

If you go in for cliff exploring, don't risk silly sorts of thrills on unknown beaches and rocks that look easy and safe, but can be treacherous if you "don't know the ropes" of the neighbourhood. When staying in unknown, remote places, it is wise to find out about the district, and make friends with one or two local people, young or older. There is no place like the village post office for learning useful tips. Local inhabitants are generally helpful if you approach them in a friendly and courteous spirit.

You know, there is a good and rough way even of getting to the top of Box Hill in Surrey. The usual approach is to go to Burford Bridge Station. From there the climb is longish if you are not used to hills, but is really easy. And the views across the Surrey Hills are lovely, so take your camera with you if you go in for snapshots. Ramblers who want a harder "pull up" might try getting to the summit by tackling the hill from the Brockham side. You could make a day of it, going first to Dorking to explore that attractive town, and from there loop back to Brockham by a bus you board at the lower end of the High Street. Tell the conductor you want Brockham Hill, and he will advise you to get out at the right spot, where the roads bend and fork. At the foot of Brockham Hill stands a rambling, old country house with an equally rambling but delightful garden right at the entrance of the lane up the hill. It is a landmark.

Hill-climbing does not require the equipment wanted for real mountaineering, but you must be suitably clothed. Comfortable slacks are really better than shorts, for they can save you many a scratch and insect sting. Then loose, airy blouses or tops, and warm, light cardigans answer

Suitably clad, they are enjoying the delights of climbing.

After a long climb they relax at the Lizard, southernmost point on the coast.

most purposes and temperatures. Wear strong but not too heavy shoes. Corrugated foam soles are good, and do have ankle socks in the shoes. It is so much more comfortable for long walks, and you can always remove them should you find a nice spot for sun-bathing.

A small bottle of midge-repelling lotion is a good companion on such outings, and do take more than one handkerchief; paper tissue ones are best, then you won't go and lose a treasured one.

A friend of mine has evolved a refreshing idea for a hand and face clean-up. She soaks a wad of cotton-wool with water and eau-de-Cologne, wrings it, and keeps it in one of those little plastic cases. Such an aid takes little room in your rucksack.

Exploring the hills of Dartmoor is another story. If any of you visit that lovely, and in parts still untamed, area of the West country, do know your ground and your distances before venturing on an excursion.

Young ramblers should strike out in small parties, never less than three; preferably one of them should have previous knowledge of the moor if possible. Take a map and a local guide-book with you. Don't carry too much weight, for on Dart-

moor you will not want to camp out unexpectedly. But if you are on a holiday without your parents, you will tell your landlady or hostess where you are going when she gives you your sandwiches.

Take an extra scarf with you, for even on warm days the wind blows keen and strong on top of the tors. I have sat by Saddle Tor summit on an afternoon that had burnt lovely and hot down below in the heather, and yet the wind up there felt like a boisterous, ice-cold hand hitting one, in spite of the bright sun and blue sky.

The trudge up to many of the Devonshire tors is marked by a smoothly worn imprint up the close-cropped, mossy grass. Follow that imprint. It is where countless climbers before you trod you an easy path to the great granite rocks topping the steep hills. To young explorers on their first Dartmoor visit, I would say, keep near the roads, unless you have a Moor expert with you. The famous beauty spot can be as risky for the ignorant as any mountain. Lush and bright green grass in the valleys of heather and gorse and fern, denotes the vicinity of marshland. Bogs can be dangerous on Dartmoor.

Watch out for mist as well. You can be

Two of the ramblers who made the climb are seen on Snowdon's rocky slopes.

as helpless in it as if you met it on a Welsh or Scottish peak. So never continue climbing the hills or exploring a remote valley if there is any sign of mist. Weather signs can be read in the sky and felt in the atmosphere during your day's ramble.

If, when you look down from one of the hills, you see the whole landscape below you so sharply and clearly etched that landmarks appear much nearer than they really are, look out for rain, however limpid blue the sky or bright the sun. Heed that signal, be prudent and climb down to the roadways.

Stormy weather often flicks advance notices in the sky by feathery, playful-looking wisps of clouds on the blue.

Your "pony-tail" tied up with bright ribbon keeps your hair neat and tidy, but those "mares' tails" in the sky forecast untidy weather generally with rough squalls and gusts of rain. When you bear

in mind that rain on Dartmoor often turns to penetrating drizzle which next becomes impenetrable mist, you will remember my weather warnings, and will also not forget to add a feather-weight plastic raincoat in your rucksack or holiday hand-bag.

One last suggestion should you ramble "up-along, down-along" the Dartmoor hills on hot summer days, don't organize your picnic right up against one of the ancient higgledy-piggledy stone walls. And sit at a careful distance from rock bases. These spots have nooks and crannies favoured by the occasional adder.

So be careful to look around before you establish squatters' rights. Then you will not risk disturbing any of the creatures that have permanent privilege there. They may be enjoying the sunshine just like you, and they seldom go out of their way to strike unless something frightens them.

RAFFIA WORK

M. E. Robbins

RAFFIA AND BASS, AS IT IS known to gardeners—is a cream fibre obtained from the leaves of palm-trees. It is used for many decorative and useful purposes, such as the making of hats, bags, waste-paper baskets, lampshades, and table mats. In its natural form, raffia is best bought by the pound from seedsmen and gardening shops. It can also be obtained in many delightful colours from handicraft shops.

MAKING A BEACH HAT AND BAG SET

Materials required. For the hat, 9 oz. raffia; flowers for trimming. For the bag, 10 oz. raffia. Oval cardboard base, 13 inches by 5 inches.

The Hat (Illustration 1)

Before you begin, plait all the raffia; take 3 groups each of 5 strands and plait them tightly and evenly; weave in more strands when the first are used up. Keep on one side a handful of raffia for sewing.

Take one end of the plait, curve it into a ring and stitch it, using a darning needle threaded with raffia (no hole must show). (Illustration 1.) Now sew the edge of the plait to the edge of the circle, continuing until the circle measures 7 inches across; turn the plait to right angles to the circle and oversew one round for the beginning of the crown. Add three more rounds sewn edge to edge. To begin the brim, turn the plait the opposite way and oversew one round.

Make the brim as wide as you wish; fasten off by cutting the plait and oversewing the cut part to the edge of the hat at the back. Trim the hat with flowers, and add circular elastic at the back to keep the hat firmly on the head—or use ribbon. If a curved crown is preferred, start the crown in the same way, but ease the plait a little as you sew it, until the desired depth is obtained.

The Bag (Illustration 2)

Cover the cardboard base with raffia plait sewn edge to edge as before, stitching the raffia "mat" thus produced to the cardboard, with raffia. Turn the plait as for the hat brim and oversew one round; then continue sewing the plaits edge to edge up the sides of the basket until all the raffia is used up, except 40 inches. Cut this piece in half and sew to each side of the basket for

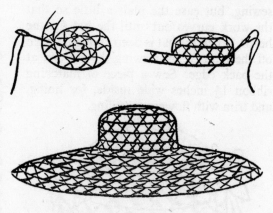

Diagram 1. Sew the plaits edge to edge for crown and oversew first round of brim. Below is the completed Beach hat.

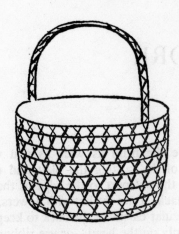

Diagram 2. Beach Bag.

handles. The bag is improved if it is lined with contrasting material.

A TOWN HAT

(Illustration 3)

Materials required. 4 oz. raffia. Trimming.

Plait the raffia, using 3 groups each of 4 strands, and keeping a little on one side for sewing. Make a small circle as before, taking care that no gap shows. Sew the plait to the edge of this circle until the work measures 4 inches across. Continue sewing, but ease the plait a little so that the work curves out until the hat fits the head. When the hat is deep enough, fasten off the plait by oversewing the cut end at the back edge. Sew a piece of matching ribbon $1\frac{1}{2}$ inches wide inside, for lining, and trim with flowers or veiling.

Diagram 3. Town Hat.

WASTE PAPER BASKET

(Illustration 4)

Materials required. 8 oz. raffia; bundle of clothes line. Cardboard base, 8 inches diameter.

Take a darner threaded with raffia and oversew rope tight round the edge of the cardboard base. To do this, cover about 1 inch of rope completely; then take the

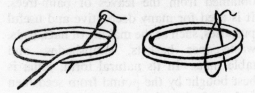

Diagram 4. How to make a waste-paper basket.

needle over the rope and right through the cardboard about $\frac{1}{4}$ inch from the edge. When the base is surrounded with covered rope, start on the upright sides.

Don't cut the rope. Continue to cover about 1 inch rope well, then take the needle under the last round, then up and over the rope, ready to cover the next inch. Continue until all the rope is covered. To fasten off, trim the end of the rope to a point, and oversew it to the top edge of the basket.

TABLE MATS

(Illustrations 5/6)

Materials required. Thick string or cord. Raffia—this varies with the number of mats to be made; start with 4 oz.

Curve one end of the string into a circle and sew, taking care that no gap shows. Thread a darner with raffia, and cover the string well. Holding the work firmly in the left hand, with the string lying along the curve, cover ½ inch of the string; then take the needle under the last round and up and over the present one (Illustrations 5/6). Next take the needle under the uncovered string and cover the next ½ inch. These long stitches, binding one round to the next, should be firm and straight. Make the mat the desired size, trim string to a point, and oversew to the edge.

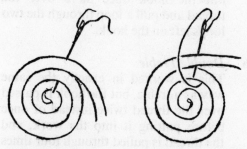

Diagrams 5 and 6. Making table mats from thick string or cord.

COVERING A LAMPSHADE

(Illustration 7)

Materials required. Wire shade. Raffia; the amount depends on the size of the shade chosen.

It is not wise to choose a shade with fancy sides, as raffia does not lend itself to curves. Cover all the wires of the sides and top and bottom edges with raffia, taking

Diagram 7. Making a lampshade.

care to go twice over the places where the wires are joined. Take a good long thick strand of raffia and sew one end of it to the top covered wire; twist the strand over to cover the cotton. Bring the strand down to the bottom edge, loop it over once tightly, then take the strand back to the top again. Repeat until the shade is completely and closely covered, always working from the outside to the inside of the shade. If liked, a narrow plait can be sewn to top and bottom edges, or fringe can be added.

HOW TO CROCHET

by Jane Koster

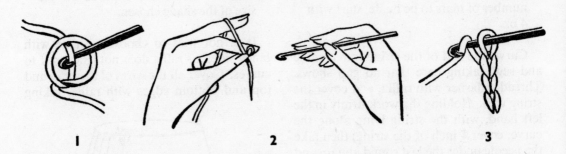

1

2

3

1. This shows you how to make a slip knot. (All crochet begins with a slip knot).

2. Hold the cotton in your left hand and the crochet hook in the right hand. Begin with a loop, which is made as we show in the picture.

3. *Chain*
Put the hook into the loop of the slip knot and then pull through another loop—this makes a chain. Continue to pull through loops for the number needed.

4. *Double Crochet*
Put the hook into the loop (as shown by the arrow) and pull another through two loops on the hook. Now

pull a loop through the two loops.

5. *Treble*
Pass the hook over the thread then put it into the loop, now put the hook over the thread again and pull it through two loops (as shown by the arrow). Put the hook once more over the thread and pull a loop through the two loops left on the hook.

6. *Double Treble*
This is worked in exactly the same way as a treble, but the hook is passed over the thread twice instead of once before putting it into the work, and the thread is pulled through four times instead of three, as when making ordinary trebles.

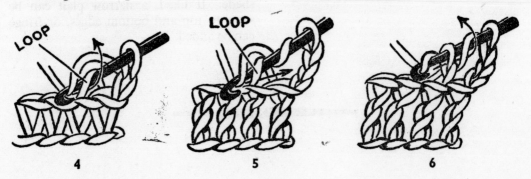

LOOP

LOOP

4

5

6

CROCHET is the partner of knitting, and everyone who wants to make knitted garments must know how to do, at least, simple crochet. Apart from trimming, crochet makes lovely fabrics for blouses and household articles, and these can be worked very simply from the stitches given here.

To learn to crochet, begin with a number 12 wool crochet hook and 3-ply wool. Make a length of chain stitches until you can work them evenly. Now turn and, leaving two chain stitches, work a double crochet into the third chain stitch. This "turn" is very important as it forms the end stitch and prevents you "losing" a stitch on every row. Work a double crochet into each chain and practise until you can work them perfectly evenly.

The next stitch to learn is "treble". This is very like double crochet, except that the thread is taken round the hook a second time and so makes it longer. Work rows of trebles until you can do them as evenly as the double crochets. The "turn" for treble must be longer than for double crochet—allow three chain stitches, working into the fourth. This will stand for the first treble of the next row.

Long trebles are worked as ordinary treble but the thread is taken over the hook an extra time and so the stitch is longer. Allow four chain for turning.

Crochet can be worked in any material —wool, cotton, silk, rayon, etc., etc. For fine work use steel hooks and for coarse, bone or aluminium. Very big hooks for shawls, etc., are sometimes made of wood.

Tension is as important in crochet as it is in knitting, so check yours carefully before beginning a piece of work. Use a finer hook if your tension is too loose and a coarser one if it is too tight.

When working edgings on knitted garments use a smaller hook than usual so that the work is very close. Loose crochet on edges is untidy and spreads the knitted fabric out of shape.

Crochet needs very little pressing. The ideal way of finishing it is to pin it out to size on a blanket, then to cover it with a damp cloth and leave it overnight. Heavy pressing spoils the appearance by flattening the stitches out of shape.

To learn fine crochet begin with a No. 7 steel hook and No. 20 crochet cotton Practise in the same way, but *do* work in a good light—fine crochet needs close attention and should never be done when the light is poor.

You should take every opportunity of looking at old crochet, especially Irish crochet—a good deal is displayed in museums and you will see how very interesting this work can be and how it gives great opportunity for invention.

WISHES

"I should like a lovely house, full of all sorts of luxurious things; nice food, pretty clothes, handsome furniture, pleasant people, and heaps of money. I am to be mistress of it, and manage it as I like, with plenty of servants, so I never need work a bit. How I should enjoy it, for I wouldn't be idle, but do good, and make every one love me dearly."

Meg, in *Little Women*

HOW TO KNIT

Jane Koster

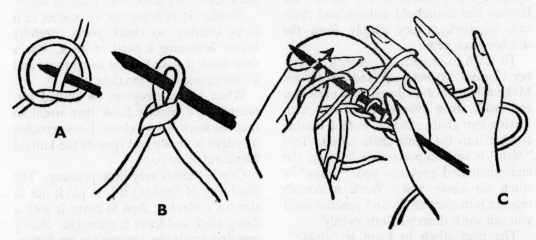

1. **(A)** Begin with a loop knot made like this.

   (B) Put in one needle and pull the loop tight.

2. *Knit Stitch*
   Holding the work as shown here, with the needle passed through the loop from front to back pass the thread round the point of the needle, then pull the loop through. Continue in this way to the end of the row.

   (C) Loop the end of the thread over your left hand thumb, then put the needle into the loop, passing the thread from the ball round the point. Pull a loop through and repeat.

   Purl Stitch
   With the right hand needle passed through the loop from back to front pass the thread round the point and pull the loop through. Continue in this way to the end of the row.

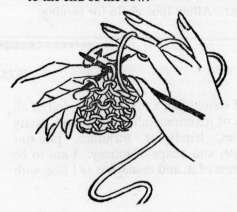

3. *Casting Off*

Knit two stitches then pass the first loop over the second. Continue to the last stitch, break off the thread and pull it through the loop.

KNITTING IS ONE OF THE OLDest crafts and one of the most useful for anyone to learn. It is easy too; there are only two basic stitches—plain and purl —all fancy patterns are combinations of these.

To learn to knit, begin with size 8 needles and 4-ply wool. Cast on 20 stitches as shown in C and knit a piece of garter stitch—that is, every row knitted in plain stitches. When you find this easy to do and your work is looking even, try a piece of stocking stitch, which is one row plain and one row purl repeated all the time. This makes a flat surface on one side of the work and a ridged one on the other. Knit a good piece of this pattern, taking care that your edges are neat.

To make certain of neat edges, knit the first and last stitches rather tightly by pulling the wool up more closely round the needle than for ordinary knitting. Always look at the first and last stitches to make sure they are neat and if necessary undo them if you think they are too loose. You will find this very important when you knit garments and have to sew up the pieces. Loose edges make the whole garment look untidy and badly knitted.

Another point to remember is to cast-off loosely. If you are making a jersey that pulls over the head, cast *on* and *off* with needles two sizes larger than you are using for the rest. For all garments you will need the beginning and ending rows to be elastic, so take care to knit them rather loosely or with bigger needles.

You will be working from instructions as your knitting progresses, and you will be given a tension to work to. This is very important, as unless you do exactly as you are told, your garment will be either too big or too small. Until you are quite certain of your own particular knitting tension, work a sample with the wool and needles given to make sure that your work is accurate. If you find your work too big use smaller needles, and if it is too small use bigger.

When you have knitted the pieces of your garment press them lightly, especially along the edges. Use a damp cloth and a good hot iron, but don't "iron" the work —just *press* it. Ironing will push it out of shape. Ribbed stitches don't need pressing unless the instructions say so and most fancy patterns are crisper if they are left unpressed.

HOW TO TAT

Jane Koster

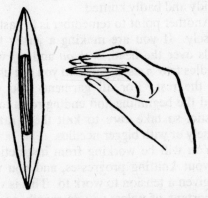

1. Here is the shuttle used for tatting—wind the cotton neatly round the centre until the shuttle is full. The shuttle is held between the finger and thumb of the right hand like this.

2. Unwind a length of cotton and hold it over the fingers of the left hand (A) to make a circle (B).

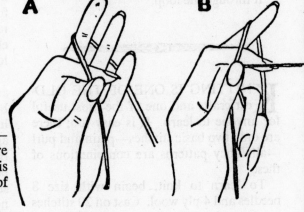

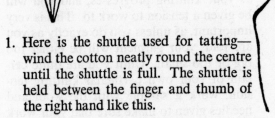

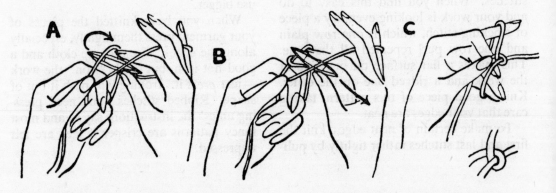

3. (A) Now pass the shuttle through the circle.
   (B) Bring it back under the thread.

(C) Use the first finger of the left hand to steady the loop. Pull it tight.

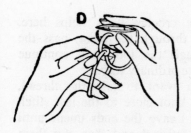
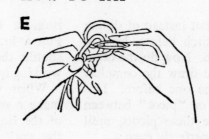
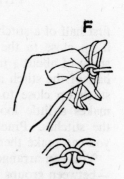

4. (D) Now pass the shuttle over the loop.

(E) Bring it back through the loop.

(F) Steady the loop with the first finger and pull the loop tight.

This makes the complete double stitch, which is the basis of tatting.

5. To make rings, work in the same way, but make the stitch on a loop from a ball of cotton instead of the shuttle thread. Little loops between the stitches are called "picots". They are made by leaving the thread loose between the stitches.

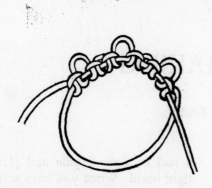

TATTING OR "FRIVOLITE" AS it was known in the last century, is a charming way of making lace edgings of all widths.

To learn tatting, fill your shuttle with No. 20 thread, wind the thread over the fingers of the left hand as shown and work the first part of the stitch from the illustration. If you have a friend who can tat, try this out with her to help you, and go on practising until you have the knack. The important thing is to use the middle finger to guide the knot on to the thread, so that it can be pushed up into place.

When you can make the knot evenly, practise making a series of loops with 16 double stitches in each. When you can do these really evenly, practise loops with picots between as follows:

Make 4 double stitches, now make the

first half of a stitch, but instead of sliding it up close to the stitch before, leave a space of about ¼ inch. Now do the other half of the stitch and draw the complete stitch up close to the one before. This makes a little loop or "picot" between the stitches. Practise these picots, until you can make them perfectly even.

You can arrange the picots as you like —between groups of 2, 3, 4, 5, or 6, etc., stitches, according to the pattern you are working. The length of the picots, too, can be varied. For a light, lacy effect, make those along the outside edge rather long and grouped together.

These picots are used for joining the rings—a fine crochet hook helps here. Pull a loop through the picot, pass the shuttle through the loop and continue working in the ordinary way.

When you want to join the thread, make a reef knot close to the last stitch of the ring. Leave the ends uncut until the work is finished and then run them into the nearest ring.

Instructions for tatting often refer to a "Josephine Knot". This is a ring made of the first half of the double stitch repeated a given number of times.

Wash tatting by squeezing it in hot, soapy water, and dry it spread out flat. It will *not* need ironing.

RUGMAKING

Jane Koster

RUGS CAN BE MADE FROM material which otherwise would be thrown away, such as old clothes, stockings, socks, etc., or they can be made from specially spun rug wool.

In the first case the material must be cut into strips about 1½ inches wide and joined to make one long strip. Keep the colours separate and wind the strips into balls to keep, until you have a good supply.

The most simple rug of all is made from plaited strips. Take three of your balls and tie the ends together, now hook them over a nail or door handle and plait a long, tight braid. When you have several plaits begin to make your rug. You will need a curved packing needle and some twine for the sewing.

Begin in the centre of the rug and sew the plaits round and round, sewing into the loops and not through the fabric. Choose the colours to make bands of contrast, cutting the braids and tucking the ends in to make complete rounds.

If you want to make an ordinary shaped rug, sew the braids together longways, tidying the ends by sewing the outside ones along the top and bottom.

To work a tufted wool rug, you will need canvas for the base and rug wool cut into short lengths of approximately 3 inches for the pile. Special gauges are sold for cutting these lengths, and it is a good idea to keep the different colours in separate small boxes so that they can be taken out as required for the pattern.

The drawings show exactly how the tufts are made. Pull each up tight as you make it, and see that the ends are even by doubling the piece of wool exactly in half before pulling the loop through.

Always allow a "turning" at each end in your canvas—two inches is enough.

Turn this over to the right side of the work so that it is doubled and tuft the two strands of canvas together.

Tuft in the same direction all the time with the unworked canvas on a table in front of you and the finished part supported on your lap. Keep the row you are working on along the edge of the table and pinch the canvas up into a ridge so that the rug hook goes through easily. Don't be tempted to do the pretty parts first—keep ploughing along, completing each row as you come to it.

The last thing is to work all along the selvedge edges of the rug, as shown in the drawing. This gives a professional finish and protects the edges from wear.

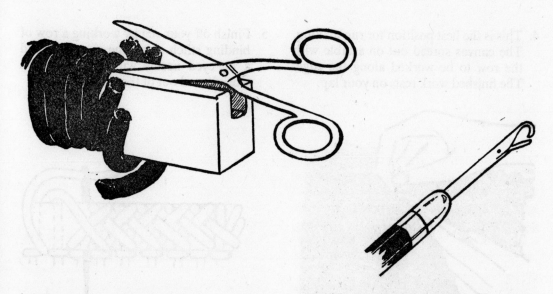

1. First of all cut your wool into suitable lengths by winding it tightly round a gauge and then cutting with sharp scissors along the groove.

2. This is the easiest kind of rug hook to use—it has a wooden handle and a metal hook and lachet—the lachet keeps the wool in the hook.

3. Spread the canvas on a flat surface. (a) Double the wool and hold it in the left hand. Put the hook under a thread of the canvas and over the wool. Pull the wool under the thread like this.

(b) Pull the loop through—the lachet holds the wool in position. (c) Now push the hook up and round the doubled wool. (d) Pull through and you have the completed tuft.

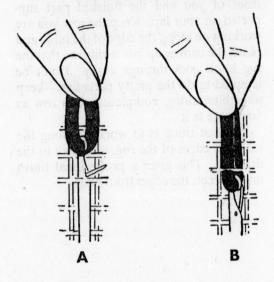
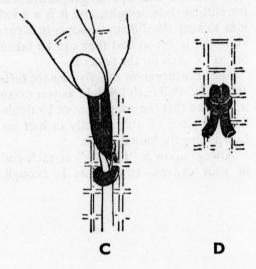

A　　　　**B**　　　　**C**　　　　**D**

4. This is the best position for rug-making. The canvas spread out on a table with the row to be worked along the edge. The finished work rests on your lap.

5. Finish off your rug by working a row of binding stitch along the sides. Thread a big-eyed needle with rug wool and work in and out of the canvas.

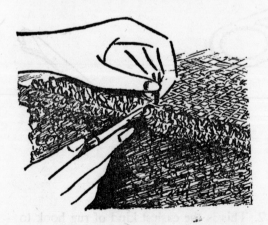
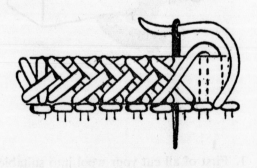

MAKING SOFT TOYS

Ruby Evans

SOFT TOYS ARE GREAT FUN TO make, for you use ordinary sewing stitches and processes to produce colourful creatures of all sizes and shapes according to your fancy. They will solve your gift problems too, not only for children, but for older friends, for you can make many of the smaller toys as pincushions, paper-weights, or just as mascots.

There is room in this craft for every-one's own taste. Some workers like to make large, sturdy elephants and dogs to please a toddler, others may prefer cuddly teddies, gollies and lambs. Perhaps you may like to specialize in dressed dolls or character animals, or you may find you have a flair for the miniature creatures which are popular as lapel-brooches.

Often your first toys will depend on what material is available, for almost any-thing firm, strong and pliable can be used. Felt is one of the most suitable, and cer-tainly one of the pleasantest materials, for it comes in many gay colours, and as the edges do not fray, it is very easy and quick to handle. It is economical too, for you can use up the tiniest scraps for trimmings.

If you haven't much pocket-money to spare for new materials, try to find some strong firm cloth, print or velvet for your first toys, washing and pressing the pieces before use. As these will sometimes be dull

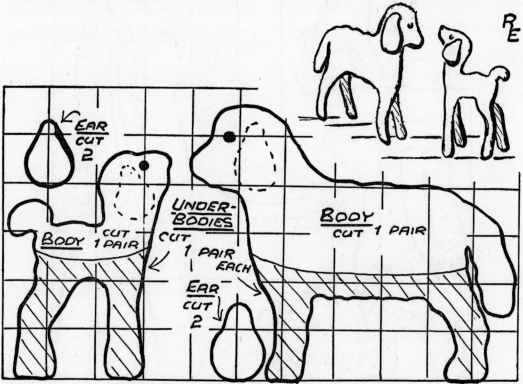

A diagram for making a sheep and lamb from flowered print.

in colour, hunt out scraps of ribbon, belts or discarded handbags to provide bright collars, shoes or ear-linings to give the toys a gay touch.

The best stuffing for small toys is kapok, but any other light-weight filling would do, but make sure that it is new and clean, and free from moth. Wadding is quite good too, especially for small toys, and you can buy it by the yard very cheaply—but use dressmaker's wadding (the kind you have in shoulder-pads), not the surgical kind. Try not to use snipped-up rags if you can possibly avoid it, for they make very lumpy, heavy toys.

When you have made a few small toys, you may like to try larger animals made from fur-cloth. You can buy these furry fabrics in many colours and styles and they make excellent hard-wearing toys, but this type of fabric is a little more difficult to handle. Furry toys can be stuffed

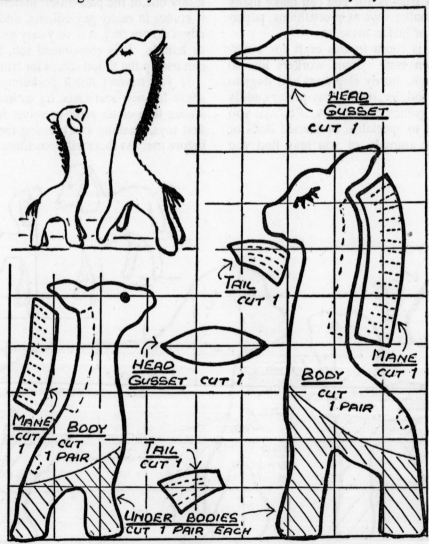

This delightful giraffe and baby can be made from yellow felt.

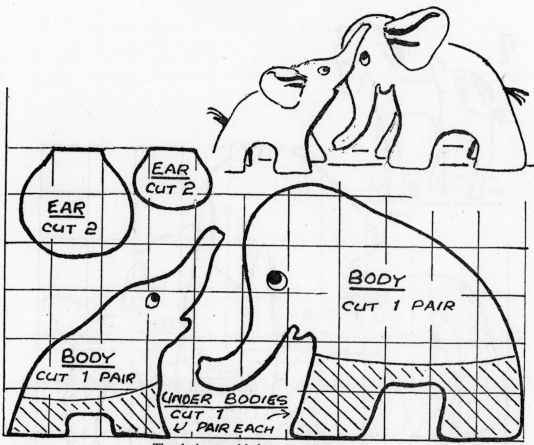

The elephant and baby are made in grey felt.

with wood wool, which is the coarse wood shavings in which china and glass is packed.

Always have a pattern, which will help you to get the true characteristic shape of each animal. There are many available, either full-size on a chart, ready to cut out, or in the form of diagrams on a squared background, as you see here. This is a very practical way of making your patterns, for by varying the size of the squares, you can make your patterns any size you like.

Large toys are usually made up on the wrong side with very strong seams, preferably back-stitched by hand with strong double cotton, and then turned right side out. Don't machine them unless you are very skilful, as the many turns and curves need great care. Small toys are best sewn up on the right side, as it is difficult to turn them afterwards.

Often the pattern tells you where to leave an opening for stuffing. If it does not, leave a space where you can reach all parts of the body easily, either across the back, in the centre of the tummy or just below the tail. The secret of good stuffing is to use a very little at a time, pushing it right into the place where you want it to go before adding more. Fill the parts farthest from the opening first. Hold the toy in the hands all the time you are stuffing (that is, don't lay it down on the table and push the stuffing in), and mould the head and limbs as you fill them.

The pony and foal are made in patterned oil-baize.

You see here four pairs of small standing animal toys, each a "family" of mother and baby, and there are diagrams for making them. If you try out some of these, you will soon get the general idea of toy-making and be ready to try out variations to suit yourself.

For the animals you see here, we used grey felt for the elephants, yellow felt for the giraffes, flowered print for the sheep and lamb, and patterned oil-baize for the pony and foal, and stitched them all with matching sewing cotton.

First make patterns from the diagrams shown here. If you draw a background of 1-inch squares, you will have mothers about 7 inches and babies about 5 inches high. You could use $\frac{3}{4}$-inch or $1\frac{1}{4}$-inch squares to give you toys in exactly the same proportions, but respectively smaller or larger.

Cut out the patterns and use them to cut out materials the number of times stated. Join each pair of under-bodies along the upper curved edges, slip this complete part between the two body sections and sew up all round, leaving a stuffing-space. For the very small toys, it is a good idea to stuff as you go, filling the head and limbs as soon as you have sewn round them.

When finished, you have four pairs of small standing animal toys.

Note that the giraffes have head-gussets to make the head more round. These are inserted between nose and ears across the top of the head, with the narrowest part to the nose.

Animals with manes may either have these cut separately, possibly in a contrasting colour, and inserted into the seams (as for the giraffe), or they may be cut all in one with the body (as for the pony). Don't fringe these until the toy is stuffed and finished, otherwise they get shabby and crumpled.

Make the eyes from a few dark stitches or tiny circles of felt or leather. Some different types of eyes are shown in the diagrams, and you can alter the expression a great deal by the shape and placing of the eyes. Sew on the ears (unless they have been cut all in one with the body), giving them a contrast colour for the linings, if you want to brighten up the toy.

BEGINNING A STAMP COLLECTION

L. N. and M. Williams

STAMP COLLECTING IS BY NO means only a boys' hobby. Many girls and women collect stamps and make excellent progress, because this is a subject calling for neatness, accuracy, and artistic taste, not to mention a thirst for knowledge, which is no male prerogative.

In the early days of philately (to give

105

stamp collecting and study its technical name) women often made stamp "snakes" and decorated table tops, plates or boxes with the little scraps of coloured paper, but those times have passed, and nowadays feminine philatelists occupy some of the leading positions in the stamp world. A woman is chief assistant to the Royal Philatelic Society, London, women conduct the sales at one of Britain's biggest stamp auctioneering firms, and the feminine element is often conspicuous among the prizewinners at international stamp exhibitions. So, with these examples before you, there is every inducement to begin a stamp collection yourself.

Stamps are the most important part of a collection, but you will need more than just stamps if you are to make a success of it. There are many different kinds of collections, and it may be best if you first consider which kind appeals most to you.

A straightforward general collection, one which incorporates postage stamps of all countries, offers plenty of scope and amusement without demanding much creative ability. A specialized collection, embracing the issues of only one country or group, can call for a large amount of your spare time, much reading and study, and perhaps in the long run a fair amount of money. A thematic collection, one based on stamp designs and comprising all issues connected with one particular theme, offers amusement, some scope for research and artistic ability.

You must make up your own mind which collection to form, but it is a good idea to begin along modest lines with a general collection. By doing so you will see and handle many different stamps which themselves may help your eventual decision.

Your first album should not be too big or expensive; on the other hand, do not start by keeping your stamps in a scrap book, a pocket book or similar receptacle. Begin with a proper stamp album, which is made especially to house specimens and keep them clean and free from damage. Many different kinds of albums are on the market, but the type best suited to your early needs is one with country headings at the top of each page and blank spaces for stamps beneath. See that the pages are fairly stiff and that the binding is of good quality. Also be sure that there are stiff guards between the pages to prevent the album from bulging badly when it is full. If the pages are printed on both sides it is a good plan, when buying the album, to obtain also some sheets of transparent interleaving paper, which you can put between heavily mounted pages and so prevent specimens on opposite sides from rubbing against each other.

To start your collection perhaps you were given some stamps by a friend or an-

---

CAPTIONS TO STAMP ILLUSTRATIONS—Reading left to right across:

1. An airmail stamp from Ireland. 2. Stamp commemorating the 100th anniversary of the first postage stamps of the Barbados, showing the old "Britannia" design. 3. Lace-making on an issue of St. Helena.

4. Stamp of U.S.A. honouring Betsy Ross, who made the first Union flag. 5. An early stamp of Great Britain, issued in the days before stamp perforation was invented. 6. A stamp issued by Bechuanaland to commemorate the Royal Visit to Africa in 1947. 7. Nurses on stamps can be the subject of an interesting thematic collection. This stamp was issued by U.S.A. 8. This triangular stamp came from the Netherlands. 9. A children's stamp from the Netherlands. 10. Eva Péron on a stamp from Argentina. 11. Mourning stamp for Queen Astrid of Belgium. 12. A typical Hungarian costume on a stamp from the land of the Magyars. 13. Refugees Organization stamp of the United Nations. 14. A Christmas stamp from Austria. 15. Princess Anne on a "Health" stamp.

other collector, but if not, or even if you were, you can form a sound beginning by buying a packet of 500 or 1,000 or more different stamps. Packets of that kind are easily and fairly cheaply obtainable; of course, the bigger the packet the more it will cost, but it is good to begin in this way and the variety of the designs, colours, inscriptions, and values will give you at once an inkling of the tremendous scope of philately. See that all the stamps are free of paper, that is to say, any which have parts of envelopes still attached to them should be floated carefully in clean, warm water, and when the gum is loosened the paper can be removed easily. The stamps can then be left to dry between sheets of clean, white blotting-paper.

Mounting the stamps on the album pages is the next process. Stamps must never be affixed to pages with gum, glue, paste, stamp edging, music tape or anything other than the specially prepared hinges which are obtainable from any stamp dealer. They are small rectangles of transparent paper, gummed on one side. To mount a stamp you lightly moisten the gummed side of the hinge about one-third of the way along its length, and affix it to the back of the stamp at the top; then bend the remaining two-thirds of the hinge backwards, so that the fold occurs just below the upper edge of the stamp. The gummed part should now be outwards, parallel with the back of the stamp. Next, dab your little finger on your tongue and lightly wet the middle of the gummed portion of the hinge, turn the stamp over, and affix it to the page where required, gently pressing it down so as to adhere firmly. When you want to turn the stamp up so as to examine its back, perhaps to inspect the watermark, you will be able to do so easily. Furthermore, if ever you want to transfer the stamps to another album they will come away without difficulty.

It will help you in your task of sorting stamps if you obtain what is known as a stamp finder, a booklet which tells you the meanings of some of the inscriptions on your specimens. A stamp catalogue, too, is very useful for the same purpose; several catalogues are published in Great Britain, and you should be able to borrow one or more of them from your local public library.

Numerous books have been written about stamps, ranging from introductory guides to advanced studies, and if you want to know more about this fascinating subject your local librarian will be able to help you by telling you their titles. There are also many magazines devoted to stamp collecting and containing interesting notes on newly issued stamps, articles on various aspects of the hobby and much information to help you on your way. If you follow the advice it should not be very long before you are a fully-fledged philatelist.

COLOURFUL MODELS
FROM FIRE CEMENT

Edward G. Smettem

ONE OF THE MANY SATISFY-ing things about modelling in fire cement, is that it is inexpensive. Not only is the material cheap to buy—from any local ironmonger—but you need no special tools. An old table knife, a pen-

A quaint little cottage made from two empty matchboxes, securely stuck together.

knife, a piece of wood on which to model —and a few odds and ends which you can find around the house—and you are set up.

With these simple things you can even make your new hobby pay, by producing, with a little practice, many attractive and useful objects to sell at your next Charity Bazaar, or by making Christmas and Birthday gifts for your family or friends. For these models in fire cement are quite permanent—just like stone or very hard pottery—when the cement is properly dried out. After treatment, which I shall describe later, you can paint them in gay colours with anything you choose—poster colours, water-colours, oil-paint, enamel, lacquer.

WHAT YOU CAN MAKE

The ability to use colour on the finished models opens up an attractive field of alternatives in what you choose to make. There are simple wall-plaques; fancy tops for jars or boxes, in relief; book-ends; model cottages, churches, etc.; animals; dolls' furniture; ash-trays; paper weights, etc., all giving you the chance to be original and use your imagination. A little patience and practice with this fascinating material, fire cement, will lead you into trying more ambitious designs.

HOW TO START

Buy a tin of fire cement from your local ironmonger or hardware store. A 1-lb. tin will cost you 1s. 6d., and a 2-lb. tin, 2s. 6d.

Moulding decorative oddments from small powder-jar lids and an empty meat-paste pot.

Ask for "Pyruma" Fire Cement (from which were made all the models illustrated here) and, in case you want to make any models with parts which require jointing together, get also a small tin of "Tiluma" Tile Cement, price 1s.

Before you begin, spread a sheet of newspaper over the table and also, I suggest, over the floor immediately under the table. The "crumbs" from fire cement are not in any way harmful, but they harden and are better cleaned away than left to tread about. Also, see that your "tools" (table knife, penknife, etc.), are to hand, plus a jar or cup of water, and a piece of rag.

"Pyruma" cement is in an airtight tin, the lid of which is to be "levered" off, and *always replaced tightly* after taking out the quantity of cement you require.

You will find that the cement is quite soft and putty-like, and easy to work in the hands. It may be, if a fresh supply, a little too soft and "tacky" at first.

A little french chalk (two pennyworth at the chemists!) or talcum powder, on the hands and on your modelling board, will help while the Pyruma is steadily drying out. (By the way—the white residue it leaves on your hands is an excellent cleansing agent—a wash will leave your skin extra clean and soft.)

BEGIN WITH SIMPLE THINGS

Roll small pieces of Pyruma into tiny balls, piercing each with a pin as you lay it aside, preferably in an old baking tin. Place in front of a fire or in an oven which is cooling off after cooking. Then you have beads, ready for grading and threading before applying colour (see note on

Finishing). The beads in front of the elephant ash-tray were made in this way— the larger ones made by rolling the cement with a circular motion under a flat piece of wood.

Now try a simple, round object like the elephant. Trunk, body, and tail are all one piece, and are allowed to harden before attaching the two ears and the four legs. These are put on while they are *plastic*, with the aid of a smear of Tiluma jointing cement, so that they can be smoothed into the contours of the body and head. The ash-tray is first shaped in solid mass, and then the centre is cut out with an inverted glass or tin—using the same "cutter" to cut a base ¼ inch thick, which is cemented in with Tiluma when hard.

MOULDING DECORATIVE ODDMENTS

This can be very effective, as shown in my examples of small powder-jar lids illustrated opposite. The lid which is on the bowl is Pyruma about ¼ inch thick, upon which has been impressed a circular mould carved in wood—and used about half a century ago for moulding butter pats!

The designs on the other two "lids" are obtained from the bottoms of a cut glass milk jug and a small glass vase respectively, impressed into Pyruma and then cut round with an inverted glass. The lid with the rose motif has been finished in Chinese lacquer, while the others are, as yet, unpainted "stone". (Incidentally, the jar in the picture is an empty meat-paste pot.)

You can mould *actual leaves* from trees and plants by impressing their *backs* into Pyruma—rolling them over with a rolling pin and letting the cement harden. From the hardened mould you can take as many "casts" as you like; then, with your penknife, cut round the edges to shape, so that you have a positive leaf that is wafer-thin.

To obtain thin sheets of Pyruma, roll it

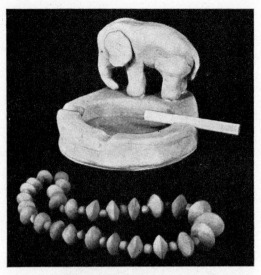

This delightful elephant ash-tray and the beads in front are some of the things you can make with fire-cement.

out between two thicknesses of newspaper, using talcum or french chalk to prevent sticking. Always chalk the sheet of cement before impressing it into the mould.

MODELLING HOUSES

Quaint little cottages, similar to the one shown on page 109, are simply made—on a "core" or frame composed of two empty matchboxes securely stuck together (including their inner slides) with Tiluma. When dry and firm WET the sides— and also wet the tip of the table knife. Then "butter" Pyruma (straight from the tin) around the four sides, to a thickness of about 1/16 inch.

Now, while the cement is still soft, impress in your window panes with the square section of a match-stick, and put in the window frames, timbering, and door, by scoring in with the point of the moistened penknife. While this is baking in front of the fire, cut the roof from solid Pyruma, scoring in the "thatch" and allowing for the overlapping eaves. This requires slow drying—gradual heat. Chimney stacks are also solid, with base slanted to the slope of the thatch, and bricks scored in. When all is hard and dry, cement together with Tiluma and heat again before painting.

FINISHING

Before you attempt to paint the models, there is a simple treatment against efflor-

escence (the exuding of salt deposit) which otherwise may occur. Give two full coats of a solution composed of two teaspoonsful of Epsom salts, one tablespoonful of vinegar in a cupful of water. Let each coat dry out before applying the next—then wipe off any salt which may appear on the surface of the model. Now you can paint with what you like.

BALLROOM DANCING

Victor Silvester

Victor Silvester

A FEW MONTHS AGO, PASSING that "dead" half-hour before the red light flashes on and you know you are "on the air" in front of the B.B.C.'s television cameras, I whittled away the time. Most

artistes have some doodling bug to which they give free rein during the minutes before a show. That evening I decided to note down all the *good* things about ballroom dancing.

Regularly we read of the bad things— years of patient, professional work from thousands of dancers are ignored in a swift flush of photographs of some new craze. "The Creep" was one recent example. Here was a sloppily-designed and performed craze which had almost nothing in common with real ballroom dancing. And yet, seemingly overnight, it became a worldwide news item.

But let me take down from my pad a few of the good things about ballroom dancing, which I detailed in that television studio.

First, ballroom dancing is a healthy, indoor exercise. You can keep in training —or keep regular hours on your entertainment—all the year round.

For tens of thousands of young people it is almost the only exercise they can get, especially in larger towns and cities. It is a social pastime, unlike, say, the cinema which is individual in that you sit passive in the dark and let yourself be entertained by others. And it is a social amenity—if you can dance it is rather like having the magic password to a well-balanced, varied leisure-time life. More than that: it's fun.

Ballroom dancing, by its very nature, promotes grace, well-groomed movement, and a bodily fitness which goes well with the natural poise which regular, good dancing soon develops. And your breathing, your digestion—both are helped by dancing's demand that the spine be straight and the body held in balance.

As a relaxation it freshens up your body and your mind. Both are likely to wilt under the routine most of us have in our daily lives, but dancing sharpens the senses and, by resting your mind, acts rather like a battery recharger. You know the old adage about all work and no play? Very few dancing "Jacks" are dull boys, believe me! They are too wide awake.

The ballroom itself is a comfortable, well-ventilated, well-lit meeting place; one of the best atmospheres in which to meet friends and make new friends. And, by its necessity of meeting new faces and making yourself conversationally interesting to varied partners, it helps in that phase known as "growing up". This stage in life has been given many names and many descriptions. I think of it much more simply as just the time when you get around to being able to meet people easily and converse with new friends generally. It's a time of fitting yourself into the life you are going to lead. No more than that. And, I think, dancing helps.

It helps because it provides companions, friends, and conversation—it gives a common interest to young people, to lonely people, to people who don't like to merely sit and have entertainment "done to them".

All over the country there are thousands of dance schools run by qualified, established teachers who belong to one or other professional organization. Here you will be taught the rudiments of what has become internationally famous as "English-style ballroom dancing".

Here you will learn the standard four ballroom dances—waltz, foxtrot, quickstep, tango—and the various others which have become popular. You will be coached in each until you can take your place on any dance floor with confidence.

By the time you are proficient it is almost invariably true that ballroom dancing has gripped your interest, not merely your feet. Something you started so as to be able to "get round the floor" will have become a day-by-day interest and hobby which you want to spend all your leisure time improving! Or so it happens in thousands of cases every year!

And few hobbies have the gradual, building-up interest of ballroom dancing.

Even now, after years of being a bandleader, I feel a thrill when I demonstrate part of my television lesson. And I have spent more hours on the dance floor than I care to remember!

For those who are interested in taking up dancing as one of your hobbies I have included the first and basic steps of the Waltz.

Through several generations the Waltz has remained popular in various forms, chiefly owing to its fascinating music and romantic appeal. The tempo of the modern version varies from thirty to thirty-two bars per minute; and it is in three-four time, which means that there are three beats to each bar. The fundamental lilt of the dance is gained by a gradual rise on to the balls of the feet through each bar and a fairly rapid lowering at the end of each third beat. Beginners will find that this lilt comes naturally to them after they have mastered the actual steps and can execute them with confidence.

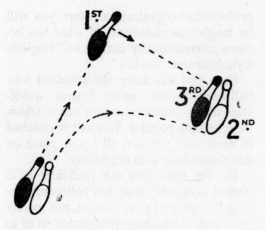

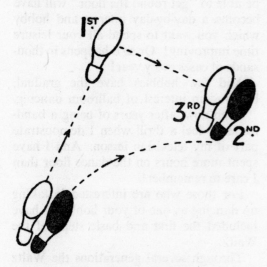

THE FORWARD CHANGE

(Starting with left foot)

Fig. 1.

MAN'S STEPS

1 Step forward with the left foot, a normal step, rising on to balls of feet at end of step . . **First Beat**

2 Right foot to side, on balls of feet . . . . . **Second Beat**

3 Close left foot to right foot, well up on balls of feet, lowering at end of step . . **Third Beat**

WOMAN'S STEPS

1 Right foot back, a normal step, rising on to balls of feet at end of step . . **First Beat**

2 Left foot to side, on balls of feet . . . . . **Second Beat**

3 Close right foot to left foot, well up on balls of feet, lowering at end of step . . **Third Beat**

At the completion of this step we are ready to proceed into the Natural Turn. But before learning this next figure practise the Change Step thoroughly until you are able to perform it without difficulty in time with the music. And adopt this same method with every figure.

THE NATURAL TURN

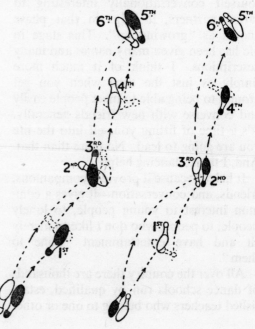

THE NATURAL TURN

Fig. 2.

MAN'S STEPS

1 Step with the right foot forward, a normal step, beginning to turn to the right, rising on to balls of feet at end of step . First Beat

2 Still turning, side left foot, on balls of feet . . . . Second Beat

3 Still turning slightly, close right foot to left foot. Well up on balls of feet, lowering right heel at end of step . Third Beat

4 Left foot back, a normal step, beginning to turn to the right, rising on balls of feet at end of step . . . . First Beat

5 Still turning, side right foot, on balls of feet . Second Beat

6 Close left foot to right foot, well up on balls of feet, lowering at end of step . . Third Beat

The man is now in a position to step forward with his right foot into a Change Step starting with the right foot, which is described after this figure.

WOMAN'S STEPS

1 Left foot back, a normal step, beginning to turn to the right, rising on balls of feet at end of step . . . . First Beat

2 Still turning, side right foot, on balls of feet . . . . Second Beat

3 Close left foot to right foot, well up on balls of feet, lowering at end of step . . . Third Beat

4 Step forward with the right foot, a normal step beginning to turn to the right, rising on to balls of feet at end of step . First Beat

5 Still turning, side left foot, on balls of feet . . . . Second Beat

6 Still turning slightly, close right foot to left foot. Well up on balls of feet, lowering right heel at end of step . . . Third Beat

At the end of this figure we are ready to proceed into another Change Step, this time starting with the right foot.

THE FORWARD CHANGE

(Starting with right foot)

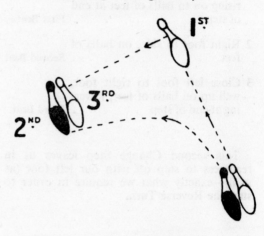

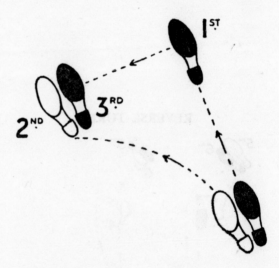

Fig. 3.

MAN'S STEPS

1 Step forward with the right foot, a normal step, rising on balls of feet at end of step . First Beat

2 Left foot to side, on balls of feet . . . . . Second Beat

3 Close right foot to left foot, well up on balls of feet, lowering at end of step . . . Third Beat

WOMAN'S STEPS

1 Left foot back, a normal step, rising on to balls of feet at end of step . . . . First Beat

2 Right foot to side, on balls of feet . . . . . Second Beat

3 Close left foot to right foot, well up on balls of feet, lowering at end of step . . . Third Beat

This second Change Step leaves us in readiness to step off with our left foot (as man)—exactly what we require in order to start the Reverse Turn.

REVERSE TURN

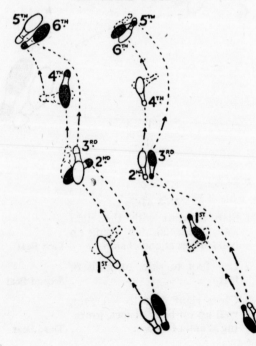

REVERSE TURN

Fig. 4.

MAN'S STEPS

1 Step forward with the left foot, a normal step, beginning to turn to the left, rising on to balls of feet at end of step . First Beat

2 Still turning, side right foot, on balls of feet . . . . Second Beat

3 Still turning slightly, close left foot to right foot. Well up on balls of feet, lowering left heel at end of step . . . Third Beat

4 Right foot back, a normal step beginning to turn to the left, rising on to balls of feet at end of step . . . . First Beat

5 Still turning, side left foot, on balls of feet . . . . Second Beat

6 Close right foot to left foot, well up on balls of feet, lowering at end of step . . . Third Beat

WOMAN'S STEP

1 Step back with the right foot, a normal step, beginning to turn to the left, rising on to balls of feet at end of step . First Beat

2 Still turning, side left foot, on balls of feet . . . . Second Beat

3 Close right foot to left foot, well up on balls of feet, lowering at end of step . . . Third Beat

4 Left foot forward, a normal step, beginning to turn to the left, rising on balls of feet at end of step . . . . First Beat

5 Still turning, side right foot, on balls of feet . . . . Second Beat

6 Still turning very slightly, close left foot to right foot. Well up on balls of feet, lowering at end of step . . . . Third Beat

SCOTTISH DANCING

Hugh Christie

ONE OF THE MOST VIGOROUS, enjoyable, and yet graceful forms of dancing—if it is done well—is Scottish or Highland dancing. And one of its great advantages is that you don't need to be an expert to enjoy it thoroughly!

It is easy to learn, as there are only two basic rhythms in Scottish dancing: *Reel time*, which is a two-bar beat, one-two-three, one-two-three—and *Strathspey time*, which is also a two-bar beat in a syncopated rhythm, one-two-three-and-four, one-two-three-and-four. There are many variations of step which can be danced by experts, but novices can manage with the two or three described below.

Once these steps are known, there are certain basic patterns, such as *reel-of-three*, *reel-of-four*, *setting* and *turning corners*, *casting-off*, *poussette*, *allemande* and *four (six, eight) hands round* which, when learned, will enable newcomers to Scottish dancing to master almost any of the hundreds of dances which come from north of the border. Nearly two hundred of these are described in excellent booklets published by the Scottish Dance Society through Paterson's Publications, Ltd., obtainable by any music shop. They are published separately with instructions and music or, with instructions alone, in six booklets of thirty-six dances each, and the whole six will fit easily into a small handbag.

There is a wide range of gramophone records to provide the music, and, as the dances are nearly always danced to tunes with the same names, they are easy to choose. The average pianist or fiddler should be able to master the music, provided she is fairly nimble-fingered, because the tunes, although not difficult, are nearly always in a fast tempo.

Here are the two basic steps, and easy ways to learn them.

1. *Reel time*. The step is called the *pas de basque*. A novice can get the rhythm by marking time with a pause in the middle: Right, left, right, pause; left, right, left, pause.

Repeat, but step to the right and left on the steps marked in italics, bringing the other foot up to the side of the first: *Right*, left, right, pause; *left*, right, left, pause. Repeat, but this time jump a little on to the foot marked in italics.

Repeat once more, this time pointing the toe of the foot marked in italics to the right and left respectively, and bringing the other foot with the heel at right angles to the firstfoot level with the instep.

This may feel a little awkward at first, especially if you turn the knee of the side-going foot as you should, but it will soon come naturally. The step should be done vigorously, but grace and neatness should not be sacrificed to vigour. Only the boy's hands should be raised; the girl's should be held loosely at the sides.

When partners do this step opposite each other (or the strathspey steps described later) they are said to be "setting" —and a set is usually followed by a turn, in which the partners join both hands, arms bent at the elbows, and swing each other round once or twice, according to the time of the dance.

REEL OF THREE: (To 1st partner):
Fig. 1. *Setting:* Step first to your own right (black arrows), then to the left (dotted arrows).

2. *Strathspey time.* Here are three steps, one progressive, two for setting.

(*a*) Progressive. One pace forward with left foot; one small pace forward with right foot, so that the right toe is level with the left heel; one pace forward with the left foot; hop on left foot, at the same time bringing up the right foot behind the calf of the left leg, so that the side of the right foot lies along the calf, right toe pointing to left heel. Repeat with the right foot. That is, pace forward with right foot, left foot level with right heel, pace forward with right foot, hop on right foot bringing left foot to right calf.

(*b*) Setting. (Simple man's step, which can be done by the "male" partners if only girls are dancing—"males" can be distinguished by wearing a band of some kind, or a handkerchief round the arm, a necessary distinction in dances with complicated patterns.) Hop four times on the left leg. Simultaneously with the first hop, point the right leg and foot to the right; with the second hop, bring the right leg up behind the left calf; with the third hop, point the right foot again to the right; with the fourth hop, bring the right foot to the front of the left leg.

Repeat, with the right leg doing the hopping and the left foot pointing to the

Fig. 2. *Two-handed Turn:* Boy dances along black line. Girl dances along dotted line towards the boy, then "sets" to him.

Fig. 3. *Setting* to 2nd partner.

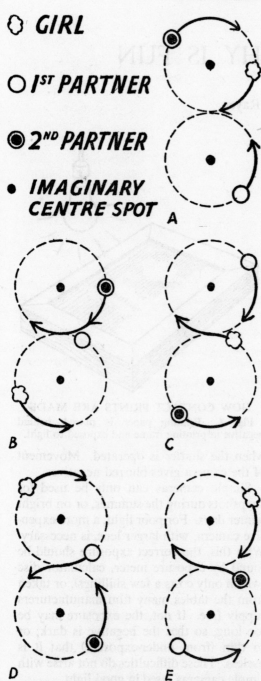

○ **GIRL**

○ **1ST PARTNER**

◉ **2ND PARTNER**

● **IMAGINARY CENTRE SPOT**

Fig. 4. A. Position at end of turn with 2nd partner. B. 1st partner about to pass between girl and 2nd partner. C. Girl again about to pass between partners on her way back. D. 1st partner about to pass between others for second time. E. All about to return to their original positions.

left, touching the right calf, pointing to the left again, and touching the front of the right leg. The change from the left leg hopping to the right leg hopping is done with a jump, and this jump is also the first hop on the right leg.

(c) The girl's normal strathspey setting step is: with the left foot slightly in advance of the right, hop twice on the left, rocking slightly forward so that the weight is on the left foot. Then, transferring the weight backwards, hop twice on the right foot.

Pass the left foot to the right, *behind* the right foot; then the right foot to the right; then the left foot behind the right again, and hop on the *left* foot (there is always a great temptation for the beginner to do something with the right foot).

Repeat with the right foot beginning. That is, hop twice on right foot, twice on left, pass right foot behind left, left foot to the left, right behind left and hop on *right* foot (again resisting the temptation to use the left foot). If in this step you seem to be dancing away from your partner, don't worry—the second half of the step will bring you back to him.

With these steps, the Scottish Country Dance booklets and a few records, most of the dances can be worked out without difficulty.

Once you have conquered the Reel Time, Strathspey, Setting, and Progressive Steps, three of you can get together and try a "Reel of Three", from these diagrams.

One final word can be added about dress. The kilt, originally a male garment, is often worn by girls now; but the most correct and becoming wear for a Scottish dance is a dress of white or some light colour with a tartan scarf (or stole, provided it does not have a fringe) passing from the right side of the waist across the breast and fastened on the left shoulder with a brooch or buckle.

PHOTOGRAPHY IS FUN

Francis G. Rayer

PHOTOGRAPHY IS AN INTEREST-ing pastime and it is always a delight to look back at snaps of places visited, or of friends, pets, sports, and hobbies. With a little care there is no reason why every shot should not be successful, the disappointment of spoilt films being avoided.

Oddly enough, the simplest, cheap type of camera is best for a beginner. With it there is then less chance of mistakes in exposure or focusing. If compactness is important, there are folding models, and also many "box" cameras, most for 12 shots 2¼ inches square, or 8 shots 2¼ inches by 3¼ inches on standard 120 or 620 film. This is a good size for beginners because contact prints are large enough for an album, while an occasional outstanding negative can be enlarged, if desired. With cameras giving very small negatives, enlargements will be required of *every* shot. This increases expense, and contact prints made at home would be too small.

Simple cameras have small lenses and shutters with one "snapshot" speed only. No focusing is necessary, all objects between about 8 feet from the camera and the far distance being sharp on the negative. So it is only necessary to wait for sunshine, or for a bright, clear day, and to snap anything not closer than about 8 feet. A good, clear print should be obtained from each shot.

A large, brilliant viewfinder is helpful, as it shows quite clearly what will be on the negative. The scene is carefully studied in the viewfinder to obtain the best view, and the camera must be held absolutely still

HOW CONTACT PRINTS ARE MADE
Fig. 1. Printing paper is placed behind negative in printing frame and exposed to light.

when the shutter is operated. Movement of the camera gives blurred negatives.

Simple cameras can only be used for snapshots during the summer, or on bright winter days. For poor light, a more expensive camera, with larger lens, is necessary. With this, the correct exposure should be found by exposure meter, calculator disc (which only costs a few shillings), or taken from the tables many film manufacturers supply free. If not, the exposure may be too long, so that the negative is dark; or so thin (from under-exposure) that it is useless. These difficulties do not arise with simple cameras, used in good light.

The more expensive camera has means of focusing, so that very near objects can be taken. For box cameras, a "portrait" lens attachment can be purchased, with

Fig. 2. Then developed for 1-2 mins. in developing solution.

similar results. With all close-up shots accurate focusing is necessary and the distance should be measured. There is less need for accuracy with distant subjects.

Printing from Negatives

Extra prints for an album, or for friends, can be made as shown. Only two chemicals are required—a developer (powder, tabloid, or a concentrated liquid to which water is added) and a fixing salt, dissolved in water, which makes the prints permanent. A simple printing frame with removable back is also necessary, and a

Fig. 3. It is then rinsed in clear water, for a few moments.

packet of contact printing paper the same size as the negatives.

All the work must be carried out in a subdued light, but a red "safety light" is not necessary. A well-shaded table-lamp in a corner is suitable, or indirect light from a second room. No *direct* light must reach the contact paper, or it will become dark all over when it is developed. Candlelight is suitable for working.

The exposure (1) is made by any bright, ordinary light, and a few trials may be

required to find the correct length of time, which depends on the density of the negative. For average negatives, about 5 to 15 seconds is usually satisfactory, with an ordinary household bulb about 4 feet away from the frame. If the print grows very black when developing begins, the exposure to the printing light was too long. Similarly, if the print is very pale, even if left in the developer a long time, the exposure was too brief. A few tests will soon show what to expect.

Fig. 4. Afterwards it is placed in fixing solution for 15-20 mins

Another method of finding the correct time is to place a piece of cardboard with a slit about $\frac{1}{2}$ inch wide over the frame, making exposures of 2, 4, 6, 10, 15, and 30 seconds, the slit being moved along to a fresh place each time. The print is then developed and will have six strips of varying density. The time which gave the best

Fig. 5. The print is then washed well in running water (about $\frac{1}{2}$ hour).

Fig. 6. Then it is dried and pressed flat.

results can then be seen at a glance. The unused printing paper, and prints in the fixing dish, should be covered each time the printing light is switched on, or it will make them grey or black all over.

Albums

To keep photographs tidy and to show them off to good advantage an album is undoubtedly best. Albums may be had in many sizes, from simple types with plain pages for small snaps, to large, decorated volumes with detachable leaves and special methods for mounting the prints. With a little care a good album can be made up from stout, tinted paper or thin card.

The manner in which the photos are mounted is important—they should be neat, level, and free from crinkles. With the simpler albums, prints are pasted directly in position with one of the adhesives sold for this purpose. Ordinary glue or paste should not be used, as it may eventually discolour the photographs. Sticky "corners" for mounting photos can also be bought. Some albums have slots or cut-out "windows" to take snaps of certain sizes, such as $2\frac{1}{4}$ inches by $3\frac{1}{4}$ inches. These are neat and poor shots can be removed and replaced by better ones at any time. Another method is to use "dry-

mounting tissue". The tissue is placed between the page of the album and back of the print, which is pressed down with a moderately hot iron.

Variety makes an album attractive. A few enlargements of good shots help, with a tasteful arrangement of vertical and horizontal prints in the smaller sizes. Unless very few photos are available they are best divided into groups: "Holidays", "School", "Games", and so on. An occasional page of coloured or tinted photographs also adds interest. A simple album can be made as shown, and has the advantage that pages may be added, or spoiled pages removed, by unfastening the ribbon. Stout, tinted paper is best for the pages, with a tastefuly coloured and decorated cover of stout cardboard.

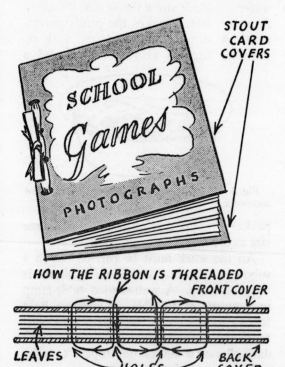

Fig. 7. An easily made Loose Leaf Photo Album.

THE GIRLS' BOOK OF POPULAR HOBBIES

A-RIDING WE WILL GO

April Jaffé

SO YOU LIKE PONIES AND FRESH air and country scenery? You want to take exercise as pleasantly as possible and with the minimum of effort? All right, you've said enough. Riding is to be your hobby; an expensive but exhilarating one.

The four essentials are: a horse, a hard hat, a pair of jodhpurs (and, of course, some birthday-cheques!) in that order. You can, if you live near the country, do what we did as children: knock at the door of every farm in the district till you find a pony that needs exercising, or a cob that still has sufficient energy left after doing its job between the shafts to give you an hour or two's lesson in the evenings or at week-ends. You'll be surprised at the number of obliging farmers and animals at your disposal.

"Yes," you may say, "but no farmer has time to teach a beginner." Agreed. Then you must pop a snappy little advertisement in the nearest local paper asking for: "Someone to teach me how to ride, for pocket-money. Pony provided." You'll save a heap of money this way, which you will need to invest in the best jockey cap or bowler you can find, and a cheap pair of jodhpurs. (Don't ride in slacks, or your knees will shortly be so sore and rubbed that you'll wish you'd never sat on a horse!). Advertising for this equipment in *Horse and Hound*, *Riding*, or *The Lady*, or even a post-card in a shop window, has in my experience yielded satisfying and economical results. You can, if necessary, also buy a saddle and bridle in this way.

But if you live bang in the middle of a big city you will have to go to a riding-school. You may be taught at first in a "covered school", where you will learn balance, the leg aids, to control your horse, rise to the trot, sit to the canter, and even to jump, (later without a saddle and perhaps with your arms crossed!).

Those of you who live in London can take a bus out to Richmond or Wimbledon and patronize one of the local stables which will take you for lovely rides over Richmond Park or Wimbledon Common.[1] Or you may venture forth in Rotten Row, but this will cost you anything from 10s. 6d. upwards for an hour. As long as you are *neatly* turned-out, with tidy hair, a workmanlike white shirt or plain jersey and flat-heeled lace-up shoes (not wedge-heeled!), you will be every bit as welcome as those in expensive tailored hacking-jackets and polished boots. But *please* don't tie a chiffon scarf over your hair! A pair of string gloves will save wear and tear on your hands, and prevent the reins slipping through your fingers in wet weather.

Once you have *learned* to ride, there are lots of ways in which you can keep in practice and at the same time meet other young people—even without your own pony—for the riding-schools and pony-clubs in many districts organize everything from gymkhanas and lectures, to rallies and pony-camps; and there are also riding-tours which cover a number of miles a day over glorious country and put up at a dif-

[1] *The British Horse Society will give you names of stables in whichever district you choose to ride.*

ferent hotel each night. To find the where-abouts of your nearest pony club, write to the British Horse Society, 66 Sloane Street, London S.W.1. Or if you would like to spend a holiday in a particular part of the country and combine it with a course of riding instruction, the same organization will give you suitable addresses.

But perhaps the idea of a riding-tour attracts you more? Then what about a pony-trekking holiday in the Highlands? If this sounds sufficiently romantic and adventurous for you, write to the Central Council of Physical Recreation, 4 Queens-ferry Street, Edinburgh, who will give you all the information you require. However, maybe you would prefer to explore the beautiful Quantock Hills or the New Forest—where the wild ponies come from —on horseback, in which case the same council will help you if you write to their London branch at 6 Bedford Square, W.C.1.

Now for a few starting-off hints. Always talk quietly to your horse before you mount and never approach him from be-hind unexpectedly, or you know what to expect! Pat his neck, give him a lump of sugar, bread or even a carrot, on the *flat* upturned palm. Have confidence—after all, even if you do take a toss (and you will!) it is unlikely that you will come to any great harm. Your mount is excep-tionally sensitive to your feelings; he senses in a moment if you are nervous, and that is the one thing that will make *him* nervous.

Remember, you are the master, and any orders you give must be gentle, but firm and decisive. Don't dither. If you aren't sure which way you want to go, stop and decide, then give a clear indication that you wish to start by a squeeze of the heels and a shortening of the reins. By that, I don't mean a tug. Just "feel" the horse's mouth enough to make him realize you

mean business. Never jerk the reins even as a punishment. It will only irritate your mount and make him naughtier. Light hands make a good rider, and after all your horse is a flesh-and-blood creature, far more likely to respond to kindly handling and a calm voice.

Always mount on the left side—left foot in stirrup, of course!—holding reins in your left hand and at the same time grip-ping the pommel, while using your right hand to grasp the cantle. You will be facing towards the horse's tail (then if he starts off, you won't get left behind, for you can haul yourself into the saddle by swinging your right leg over his back!).

You dismount on the left side too, by taking both feet out of the stirrups and lift-ing your right leg over the horse's back (be careful not to bump it, or he may jump!) so that you slide gently down his side, legs together, and end up facing towards him and still holding the reins in your left hand, while grasping the saddle with your right.

When sitting properly on the horse, you should only just be able to see the tips of your toes, your heels should be slightly down, and your elbows close to your sides.

Single reins are managed with the hands held palms downward, facing forward and fairly close together, so that the reins coming from either side run over your littlest finger and *under* the next three fingers, which then grip them firmly be-tween your thumbs. When ready to ride off, the remaining length is allowed to hang neatly down over your mount's left shoulder.

To turn your mount to the right, tighten the right rein and press your *left* heel back against his side. For opposite direction, process reversed.

If your pony shies, hang on with your knees, not your hands!

If you fall, *let go of the reins*. (To avoid being trampled on.)

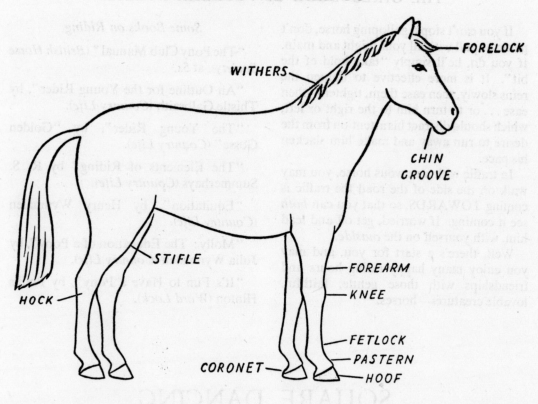

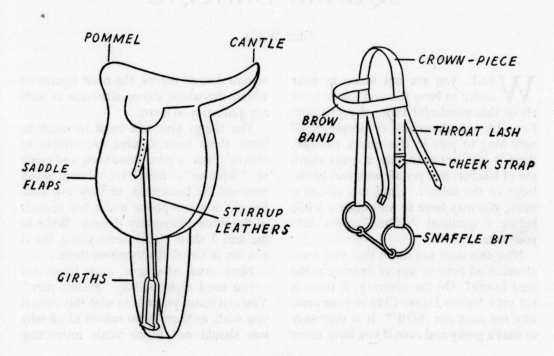

125

If you can't stop a galloping horse, don't panic or pull with all your might and main. If you do, he'll simply "take hold of the bit". It is more effective to tighten the reins slowly, then ease them, tighten—then ease . . . or to turn him to the right or left, which should distract his attention from the desire to run away and make him slacken his pace.

In traffic with a nervous horse, you may walk on the side of the road the traffic is coming TOWARDS, so that you can *both* see it coming. If worried, get off and lead him, with yourself on the *outside*.

Well, there's a start for you, and may you enjoy many happy riding hours and friendships with those gentle, faithful, lovable creatures—horses.

Some Books on Riding

"The Pony Club Manual" (*British Horse Society*), at 5s.

"An Outline for the Young Rider", by Thistle Galbraith (*Country Life*).

"The Young Rider", by "Golden Gosse" (*Country Life*).

"The Elements of Riding" by R. S. Summerhays (*Country Life*).

"Equitation", by Henry Wynmalen (*Country Life*).

"Molly: The Education of a Pony", by Julia Wynmalen (*Country Life*).

"It's Fun to Have a Pony", by Phillis Hinton (*Ward Lock*).

SQUARE DANCING

Nina Wilde

WELL, you are not alone in your desire to have fun and know more about this wonderful form of recreation. For, although thousands of people of all ages long to join in this merry pastime, there is still, unfortunately, a great shortage of teachers and people with real knowledge of the subject. Until this situation eases, you may have to wait quite a while before a qualified "caller" comes into your area.

Now this does not mean that you must abandon all hope of square dancing in the near future! On the contrary, if there is not yet a Square Dance Club in your area, why not start one *NOW*? It is very easy to start a group and even if you have never

square danced before, the basic figures on which the whole dance structure is built are quite easy to learn.

The things you will need in order to learn these basic figures are simple to obtain. First, a good handbook and guide to "Squares"—there are several good ones on the bookstalls, at very low cost. Second, a gramophone and a few records of the more elementary dances. Write to me and I shall gladly send you a list if you are in any difficulty about these.

Next—and, of course, most important —you need eight willing "guinea pigs". You can count yourself in with this eight if you wish, as there is no reason at all why you should not dance while instructing your friends. Do try to get an equal number of boys and girls if possible; although girls do very often take the parts of boys it is better (and less confusing), when learning, to have four couples.

Now let us place the four couples in position. The head couple (or No. 1) stand with their backs to the music and the 3rd couple (or No. 3) will face them with about six feet space between. When the "caller" or instructor calls "HEAD COUPLES" he means these two couples. On the right of the first couple, and facing centre, stand the 2nd couple (or No. 2) and immediately facing them are the 4th couple (or No. 4). If the caller says "SIDE COUPLES" he means these two couples.

Each boy must keep his partner on his right side, and it is most important to remember this after "swinging". The girl on the left of each boy is "the corner lady".

Now let us learn a few basic movements and make up a dance. As you will see on page 129 the first thing you have to learn is "allemande left". To do this, all the boys face their corner ladies and all give *left* hands in an upward hold. Now, walk all round your corner girl (and she will walk round you), taking eight steps. You should now be back in your "home" position.

Let's now do this movement with our own partners. Face your partner and all give *right* hands in an upward hold. Walk all round your partner, turning her with your right hand and taking eight steps to get back to place. This is called an "allemande *right*", as you see in the next picture. If the caller says, "Turn your partner with the right-hand round", he means an "allemande right". If he says, "Turn your partner with the left hand round", he means "allemande left". See Fig. 2 on page 130.

You will find that there is plenty of "swinging" in square dancing. If you

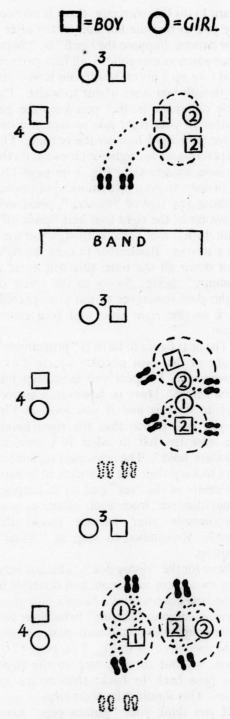

The Sioux City Sue Square Dance.

learn to do this correctly, there is no need for you to become hot and weary after a few dances. Suppose the "call" is, "Swing your partners everyone": all face partners and take up a normal ballroom hold—just as though you were about to waltz. The only difference is, that you keep the girl farther to your right side so that you can place your right foot on the outside. The girl also places her right foot forward on the outside, exactly as in Fig. 3 on page 130.

In order to get a nice smooth swift swing without any sign of "bounce", press well down on to the right foot and "push off" with the left foot—just as though you were on a scooter. Remember to keep the right foot down all the time; this will avoid a "bumpy" swing. Swing to the count of eight; then remember to put your partner back on the *right* side, and face centre again.

The next figure to learn is "promenade" —one of the most popular square dance movements. I expect you have seen this done before. There is, however, a correct way to do this and if you look at Fig. 4, you will notice that the right hands are *over* the left in what is known as "skaters' hold". The boys must remember here to keep their left shoulders in toward the centre of the "set" and try to keep an equal distance from each other, as you "promenade your partner round the town". Remember to stop at "home" position.

Now for the "docey-doe". This is a very easy movement to execute and certainly it it the best-known of all. Simply face your partner—or your "corner" (whichever the caller commands)—and walk past, passing right shoulders (as in Fig. 5 on page 131). Then, without turning, step to the right and pass back to back; then return to place. This should take eight steps.

If you think your "guinea pigs" have now learned these five movements, what about making up a dance from these figures?

Do this first without music; just count or, if you have an audience, let them clap steadily. Try to make all the things you do add up to eight counts. Let's "square our set", then, for this simple little dance.

Oh, it's allemande left, that corner girl
You make it nice and neat.
Docey-doe our own little
pearl (partner)
And don't step on her feet.
Oh, swing your partners round and
round
And I'll tell you what to do:
You promenade your partners, boys,
Just walk round two by two.
When you get home, now what do
you do?
You swing her and she'll swing you.

Repeat another three times.

You can see how very easy it is to make up a little dance like this. Even with just these five figures, a number of different routines can be thought up; as you see, although I have just made up this one I still have not used allemande right or docey-doe the corner. Of course, as you get clever you'll learn to change partners. For instance, you "follow" this call: "Allemande left and allemande right . . . Now swing with your *corner girl*, then put her on the *right*".

You will find your corner girl has become your partner and you have a new corner girl. So, if you repeat this call another three times, you will get your own partner back. Try this one—it really is great fun! All the girls keep moving one place to the right until they are back home.

Square dancing is a fine open-air recreation, so if you have a yard or, better still, a piece of lawn, what could be better? How about roping Dad in to do the calling? He'll love every minute of it—especially if he was a sergeant major at one time—and make you "hop to it"!

Sioux City Sue. Square dance
CALLS:

Fig. 1

The 1st couple right and circle four.
Yes, circle four hands round.
(No. 1 couple go to No. 2 couple and circle to the left with them—once only.)

Fig. 2

Now docey-doe the opposite girl,
That lady once around.
(No. 1 gent docey doe with No. 2 lady. No. 1 lady docey-doe with No. 2 gent.)

Fig. 3

Docey-doe your partner and then swing her, too.
Both men swing now—swing Sioux City Sue.
(Partners face each other and docey-doe. Then these two couples swing.)

———

This routine is repeated by the 1st couple with the 3rd couple, and then the 4th couple. Therefore the call would next be:

On to the next and circle four, etc.

Then the whole routine is repeated by the 2nd couple, and then the 3rd and 4th couples, in turn. See diagram on page 127.

Fig. 1. The first thing to learn is the "allemande left"—all giving their left hands in an upward hold.

G.P.H.—F*

Fig. 2. The "allemande right" all giving their right hands in an upward hold.

Fig. 3. The correct way to swing in square dancing is shown here.

Fig. 4. The next figure to learn is "promenade"—one of the most popular movements.

Fig. 5. In the "docey-doe" face your partner and walk past, passing right shoulders.

Highland dancers competing in the Sword Dance at the Aberfoyle Highland Gathering.

Four bonny lassies in the Open Reel of Tulloch.   A close-up of two dancing the Reel of Tulloch.

CYCLING

Eileen Sheridan

NINE GIRLS OUT OF TEN, ON reaching the age of twelve or so, start to pester their parents for a bicycle, and if it is at all possible for this request to be granted, the parents will be enabling their children to enjoy a sport which is not only health-giving, but which also broadens one's outlook, and teaches self-reliance. With eighteen years' experience behind me of cycling in all its aspects, I hope that what I have to say will be of benefit to my readers.

In the first place, after the initial outlay in purchasing a bicycle, the upkeep is extremely reasonable, being restricted generally to the renewal of tyres—and this only after many thousands of miles, provided they are kept well pumped up.

Many non-cyclists when told of the distances I cover on my record rides are frankly incredulous, imagining it impossible for a woman to cycle 250 miles in 12 hours, or 442 miles in 24 hours. Such rides, of course, are the result of stamina built up from my earlier touring days, combined with the speed acquired by constant racing. It is possible, however, for the average girl to cover fifty or sixty miles per day without feeling exhausted at the end, and I am talking about beginners now.

See that your machine is not overgeared to start with. Ask your local cycle dealer to work this out for you, if you don't understand gear ratios. It will only mean changing your cog on the rear wheel, and you will find a 60 to 65-inch gear quite high enough in the beginning. This is a most important point, for too often have I seen girl cyclists plodding into a wind with too high a gear. It is this fault which gives many people the impression that cycling is hard work and unsuitable for girls. A machine suitably geared requires only a moderate expenditure of energy, thus enabling the rider to maintain an even, rhythmic pedalling action.

Let us assume that you are starting off on your first long ride. You have a suitable bicycle complete with cape, puncture outfit, spanner, and screwdriver, and just to be on the safe side, it is most important to pop into your saddlebag a block of chocolate or a few sandwiches, as a stand-by against the very severe hunger which can strike at a cyclist and make the strongest person feel utterly miserable. If you remember to eat before you become really hungry you will never suffer this unfortunate feeling.

My happiest cycling memories have been of club riding, when I have explored Britain's glorious lanes with the jolliest of companions, and every moment has been enjoyed to the full. I feel a great sense of achievement on arrival at my chosen destination, and the knowledge that I have travelled there under my own "steam" always fills me with elation. Perhaps the greatest thrill of all is to reach the summit of a really lofty hill or mountain pass after a long climb, to see the countryside spread out far below you, and to feel that you are on top of the world. Then follows the exhilarating swoop down, with your hair

At the start of the Land's End to London Record, 1952. *By courtesy of "Cycling"*

There are hundreds of cycling clubs all over the country which cater for the enthusiastic club girl, whether she has in mind touring, road, or track racing. Many of these clubs have a club room where once a week you can meet your friends for a chat or a game of table tennis, and when possible a cycling film is shown—this always attracts a full house.

If you decide to become a member of a racing club, and you mention to the racing secretary that you are interested in trying a spot of speed work, you will find that you will be entered for the club's first time-trial over a possible distance of ten miles, and before you know where you are, you will probably be in the club team, regularly racing and enjoying it.

Don't be depressed if, to commence with, your times are not first-class. Remember that even the champions had to

streaming in the wind, and the road rushing beneath your wheels.

If you feel you would like company on your rides, you cannot do better than ride with your local Cyclists' Touring Club section. You can join this organization by writing for application forms to the Cyclists' Touring Club, 3 Craven Hill, London, W.2. There are generally "slow" and "fast" sections so that beginners can ride well within their capabilities, until they eventually find that they are ready for the "hard-rider's" section, where a greater mileage is covered.

Hostel week-ending is grand fun, and once a member of the Youth Hostels Association, you can spend a holiday touring at very reasonable cost. Many of these hostels are magnificent houses in famous beauty spots, and are well worth a visit. If you are interested, you can write to the Youth Hostels Association, Welwyn Garden City, Hertfordshire.

Eileen Sheridan during one of her Record-breaking runs. *By courtesy of "Cycling"*

Eileen Sheridan takes part in a Track Race.

start at the beginning and gradually you will find that your strength and stamina will increase, and your times will become faster provided you train regularly. If you are set on a racing career, special lightweight wheels and tyres are essential, but these are somewhat expensive. They are well worth the outlay, however, especially if you have your eye on championship events—and why not?

The national road racing body, the Road Time Trials Council, holds championships for women over 25, 50, and 100 miles, and also a British Best All-rounder Competition—this being a contest to find the fastest average speed over those three distances.

Naturally the competition is extremely keen indeed, and apart from the individual championships, there are team championships over the same distances.

At the finish of any of these events, club girls wait at the result board wondering which club will be the team winners, and believe me, the excitement is tense as they wait for the last girl to come in.

For the devotees of track racing there are the National Sprint, and Pursuit Championships run by the National Cyclists' Union.

Some day we are hoping for International Competition and participation in the Olympic Games, because there are many countries possessing keen racing girls, so perhaps it will not be long before we can claim a World or an Olympic Champion.

With a bicycle you need never have a dull moment, and I should like to wish you all many happy cycling miles.

Frog girl, Sylvia Gregg surfaces with a flat-iron on a Paddington stretch of the Grand Union Canal.

Sylvia Gregg is having her equipment fastened. She is wearing a rubber suit with frog flippers and a helmet with breathing equipment.

Two girls of the Aqua Club: Sylvia Gregg (left) helps Mary Maltby into her frogman suit.

UNDERWATER SWIMMING

Sylvia Gregg

UNDERWATER SWIMMING IS not altogether a "new" sport. But after the Polynesians, the Greeks and the Romans had all practised it, it was "lost" for several centuries. So it is only in the last ten years or so that more and more people have discovered the underwater world on our doorstep.

And what a fascinating place is this underwater world. There are fish that are as inquisitive as they are colourful, glowing seaweeds, mysterious caverns and, above all, the shot-silk canopy that is the surface of the water seen from below.

To reach this underwater world, one needs, as an introduction, a glass-fronted face mask, a breathing tube about 18 inches long, and a pair of rubber flippers for the feet. The mask does away with the blur which one usually associates with opening one's eyes under water. The breathing tube enables one to breathe with one's face below the surface and the flippers need only a gentle kick of the legs to send one gliding along with the minimum of splash to disturb the fish.

A set of this equipment costs about three pounds. Flippers come in three sizes, usually, small, medium, or large. There are various designs, but remember that the more pliant the rubber, the harder one has to kick one's legs, so a rigid-type flipper is the best for general underwater swimming. When buying a face-mask, hold it over your eyes and nose and take a deep breath. If, when you take your hand away, the mask sticks in position, you can be sure it will be watertight when you wear it in the water. Dipping flippers in water before wearing makes them easier to slip on, and do the same to the face-mask to prevent it misting over.

This simple equipment suffices if one does not want to be really a part of the underwater scene, for you can look in on it and dive down for half a minute or so. But if you want to feel the magic of "weightlessness"—when swimming under water resembles the flying one experiences in dreams—then you will need to use an aqualung.

The aqualung is a cylinder of compressed air with a special valve which feeds air to the breather at a pressure equal to that of the surrounding water. To explain that more simply: water is heavier than air, therefore the deeper in water one goes the greater the weight, i.e., pressure, of water surrounding the diver. So with the aqualung supplying air at the right pressure, the diver is as much at home under water as she is in her own back garden.

Let's see what it is like to go down in an aqualung for the first time. For example, over the side of a boat anchored off the Devon coast. You climb down the ladder to the sea bed. For a moment it seems impossible that the heavy cylinder (it becomes slightly buoyant in water) on your back will really allow you to breathe under water. Then you hear a noise, the "wooble" of air bubbles escaping to the surface as you actually *breathe*.

At the same time you notice the silence and the green dusky world all about. A hesitant flick of a flipper and you glide across the flat, ripply sand to a tower of rock looming darkly ahead. Round the rock is a miniature valley of red and bright green and yellow seaweed waving gently in the flow. A school of tiny fish dart through a pillar of sunlight. And suddenly, right up to your face mask swims a large fish, a mullet, probably, as though *you* were in the aquarium and *he* the six-penny visitor.

This experience is so surprising the first time that you will probably surface immediately, anxious to tell the world about it.

And once you have been underwater, you will want to go back.

Although the aqualung is an intricate piece of mechanism, it does not take more than a few hours' study (even for the most impracticable of us) to learn how it works.

A cylinder of air lasts about 45 minutes in ten feet of water and correspondingly less the deeper one dives.

There is a great deal of scope for those who do venture below the surface. Exploration is always exciting. Especially mapping the offshore coastline, the places where visibility is always good, where particular fish and seaweed, and, if one is lucky, medieval wrecks, are to be found.

Photography is another facet of underwater "work". A waterproof and pressurised camera case costs about twenty pounds. And those who start now on underwater photography have an interesting and profitable future before them. Hunting with a harpoon gun (but, please, without an aqualung), archaeology and marine biology are some other pursuits for underwater swimmers.

Although a number of people shudder to think of swimming underwater round the British coast and say that there is not enough of interest under our waters, this is quite untrue. The south, west, and north-east coasts have some fascinating waters with a multitude of fish, a petrified forest and even a wreck from the Spanish Armada. And if you dislike swimming in our waters, anyway, there are skin-tight rubber suits which keep one warm and snug for literally hours.

The unfortunate part about serious underwater swimming is the cost: forty pounds for an aqualung plus the cost of recharging air cylinders. But it is something that is really worth saving for and in the meantime a lot of fun can be had with just the breathing tube, mask, and flippers.

Incidentally, girls are particularly well-equipped for underwater swimming, as they have a layer of protective fat covering their bodies which helps keep out the cold. And the chief physical requirement is to have clear tubes between nose and ears—otherwise pressure of water can affect the ear drums. So don't go diving with a cold in the head!

If you want to know more about underwater swimming the British Sub-Aqua Club exists to further all forms of underwater activity and to train members in the use of the aqualung. The club also organizes underwater expeditions and members can use club equipment, merely paying for the compressed air they use, at a reduced club-rate. The address of the club is: 74 Lonsdale Road, London S.W.13.

COLLECTING—A LIFETIME HOBBY
Janet Lindsay

WHEN WE READ OF FAMOUS collections—valuable china, paintings, old manuscripts and so on—we seldom consider how they all started. Yet, at your age, perhaps, someone was lucky enough to be given, or come across, one single item which was so fascinating that it began a lifetime hobby.

Perhaps you have already started a collection? If not, here is a fascinating hobby and one which may one day even be lucrative. In the meantime, it will give you hours of pleasure, bring you into contact with interesting people, and add further zest to your life in the excitement of hunting for the next specimen to add to your collection.

The late Queen Mary was an inveterate collector and this year there was an exhibition of her treasures, which were many and varied. In her case, it was certainly a lifetime hobby and she made many friends among the art and antique dealers in London.

The oddest things are collected! History shows that many of the strangest collections became famous and valuable.

Try to think of something that is different from the collections of both the famous and those of your friends. At the moment, there is a craze for collecting cheese labels. You can go one better than that! Look around your own vicinity. If, for instance, you live in, or near, Nottingham or Buckingham, where lace has been made for generations, try to start a collection of lace bobbins. There is a fascinating history attached to many of them—particularly those which have burned-in inscriptions; for example, "Love from Will", "To dear Aunt Emily", or "For my Jenny"—all telling some story of love and affection between people who worked together long ago, making the beautiful lace which has outlasted them. One bobbin, still in circulation somewhere, even tells the story of an unpopular employer who was hanged, and whose workers were so relieved that they celebrated with a party and an orgy of bobbin-messages!

That is the kind of collection which you might start and which will, in time, add to your knowledge of your own surroundings and possibly become extremely valuable.

There are millions of stamp-collectors. Stamp-collecting can be a never-ending source of pleasure, learning and fascination, but many people have not the patience to make it either interesting or profitable. Study the colour and history of stamps, look for mistakes in the printing (this makes the stamp more valuable) and so on. But if you haven't the analytical type of mind, or the right temperament for stamp-collecting, try something else.

Collecting dolls from different countries is ideal for girls—if you can travel, or have friends abroad. Old dolls make an easier collection because you can search in the antique or junk shops for them. You can also enjoy repairing them and dressing them in the correct period dresses, from odd scraps of material.

If someone gives you a miniature china doll or animal, here's your chance to start a collection. Eventually you will be able to own a glass-fronted cabinet and display your collection—but be sure, before you begin, that washing china is something you like doing!

Old china, of course, needs careful handling—and some careful study. You may decide to start a collection of old Chelsea or Dresden china, which, if you choose carefully, can be built up into something valuable as well as beautiful.

Stick to one kind of china and study every book you can find which tells you its history, its special markings, how to detect fakes and repairs, and so on. Many antique dealers themselves don't know when a piece of china has been "doctored", or repaired in such a way that its real date is obscure. So here, again, you will need patience and concentration!

Seek the advice of someone who is a genuine expert on your particular choice

Collections you can make: A matchbox label, a china cat, a holiday card, a Dresden china tea-kettle and a cheese label.

of old china. He will tell you if the colour of a Dresden-piece dress marks it as a fake—or if the tree behind a Chelsea piece has been added . . . or if a god and goddess (for example, Venus and Adonis) are perfectly matched.

Learn to bargain, too. Many a fake is priced highly, while a genuine piece can be bought for a ridiculously low price—but you can't bargain until you *know*. So, first study what you wish to collect.

A less expensive hobby is collecting match-box labels. Two famous collections in this country contain over 40,000 different labels—and a man who lives in Berlin has over 90,000!

There is a lesson in this. Don't start *any* collection until you have decided that you want quality rather than quantity. It is too easy to collect feverishly and then shudder at the work to be done: *What on earth am I going to do with all these stamps, labels, etc.?*

If a collection of "hundreds and thousands" is your choice, then first plan methodically the books or cases in which they are going to be kept, mount them as soon as they are collected, and write in the details.

Postcards can make an interesting collection, especially if you use only those you receive through the post (a very inexpensive hobby!) and add relevant details: "This is where my pen-friend, Lola, lives —I mean to go to Madrid one day". "Lake Windermere—(add a quotation from one of the Lake poets)." "Grindelwald, Switzerland—I'll skate on our local rink this winter, until I can go out there and enjoy the winter sports."

You can gather from this, that hobbies make you want to do other things—and why shouldn't you? Collecting is always a link with people and places and things—always a way of adding to your own ambitions and happiness.

From postcards, we can go on to something even more interesting, Why not start your own Art Collection? There are postcard reproductions of the works of both Old Masters and contemporary artists. Details are printed on the back, which you can write neatly under each card. In this way, you can become quite learned about art and, later in life, buy large reproductions (even originals, if you become wealthy enough—and you *may*!) of your favourites, to adorn your own home.

Use your imagination—think of something out of the rut and start an original collection. There will be happy hours ahead and perhaps one day you will even find your collection famous!

PATCHWORK—A "CRAZY" HOBBY

Jane Godwin

PATCHWORK HAS LONG BEEN one of my own hobbies—ever since I inherited, along with a grandfather clock, four patchwork quilts which had been worked by my great-grandmother.

The quilts were then in need of repair, so I began my collection of "bits and pieces", begging from my dressmaker, friends and neighbours—and cutting away the best pieces from discarded summer frocks and chintz covers.

Then, because I sometimes write fashion articles, I was lucky enough to be sent samples of gay prints and chintzes. I was as thrilled as if I had been awarded first prize in a competition, as my "piece bag" filled up.

I knew that there are several kinds of patchwork, but, being a beginner, I thought any of these would be easy. But when I looked at all those pieces, when I tumbled them out of my bag, I began to have qualms!

Here, obviously, was a job that needed some planning. I must, at least, equal my great-grandmother in her sense of colour and design and, with a greater variety of fabrics at my disposal than could ever have been available to her, I should really improve on the originals.

The two popular methods, in her day, were "piece" and "appliqué" patchwork. I decided to try "piece" because I felt it would be easier to work out geometrical designs that would fit as I went along, rather than risk "crazy" (appliqué) work with shapes and sizes all different.

So I started with the popular hexagon design—and I advise you to do the same.

Next, I had to decide on colour mixing. The best way to do this is to lay out all your pieces on the floor and then pair them: plain with printed designs; neutral colours with bright colours; quiet patterns with bold ones—and so on.

Then I had to consider the weight and texture of the fabrics. Cotton and linen could not be combined with silk or velvet; a lightweight material would not stand the strain of being attached to a heavy one. My more exotic pieces would have to be put aside for a different purpose—a handsome cushion cover, curtain borders or an evening bag.

Then there were those pieces from older materials. Would *they* stand the strain? I pressed all materials with a warm iron, then tugged the cotton pieces and rubbed the silks between finger and thumb. Those which showed tiny cracks and broken

threads were discarded. (Incidentally, the pile of velvet can be revived by holding it over the steam from a kettle of boiling water).

Next, I examined the old quilts which were originally patchworked with strong cotton materials. I chose strong cotton pieces—and colours to tone with the originals, so the first part of my planning was done.

Here is the hexagon design which I used, and which you will find very easy to follow. It can be used for making simple things—a cushion cover, for instance, is a good start for the beginner but, if you have enough pieces, this can "grow" into a quilt! That is the fascination of patchwork—you never know what you will end up by doing!

The hexagon (diagram A)—or any other design—needs a master pattern. This is called a "Template". You can make one from cardboard (or an old playing card), but if you want to use it many times, make it from plywood or plastic.

I made my first one by placing an inverted glass tumbler on cardboard. I then drew a circle (as shown in diagram A) and marked out the hexagon inside it, each side of the hexagon measuring one inch. (Our great-grandmothers, who had time for fine needlework, often used hexagons with only $\frac{1}{2}$-inch sides).

Squares, diamonds, oblongs, and three-corner shapes—any geometrical shape—can be drawn for your master pattern. If you use an octagon shape, you will, of course, need small diamond patches to fit in between the bigger patches (see diagram B).

Use the master pattern on a large sheet of strong brown paper and cut out the duplicates *very carefully*. It is necessary to be accurate because, when you come to sewing the pieces together, each hexagon must fit perfectly into the next.

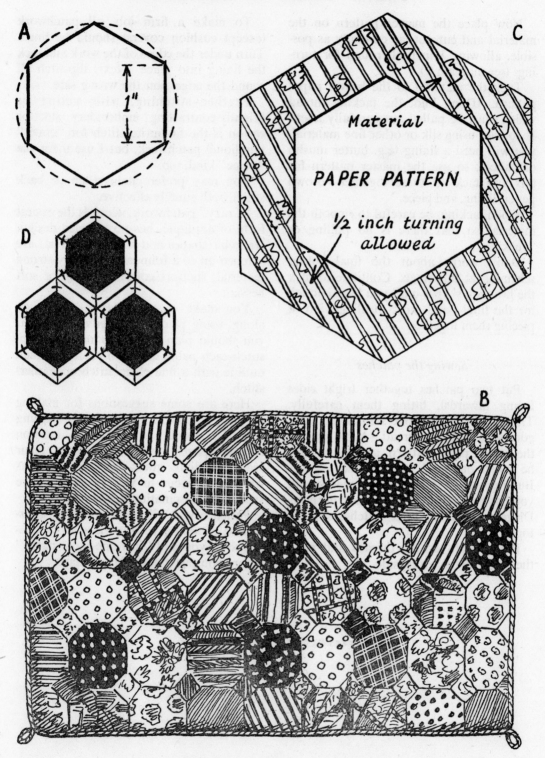

A

1"

C

Material

PAPER PATTERN

½ inch turning
allowed

D

B

Now place the master pattern on the material and cut out, as carefully as possible, allowing ½ inch all round for turnings (see diagram C).

Tack the material to the brown paper pattern. (Don't knot the tacking thread which must be pulled out carefully later). If you are using silk or other fine material, you will need a lining (e.g. butter muslin or calico), so use the master pattern for this and tack all three together—brown paper, lining, and piece.

When tacking, be careful to smooth the material so that there is no pulling or "rucking".

Don't worry about the final colour scheming at this stage. Continue to tack the hexagon shapes until you have enough for the final—and most thrilling—job of piecing them together.

Sewing the patches

Put two patches together (right sides facing inwards), fitting them carefully. Then oversew along one side of the hexagons with a strong thread. Avoid tearing the brown paper pattern, as later it must be taken out (and may be used again). Build up round these first two pieces until you have enough fabric for your purpose. Diagram D shows three patches stitched together.

Remove all tacking threads and press the fabric on the wrong side.

To make a firm job, all patchwork (except cushion covers) should be lined. Turn under the edges of the work and tack the lining into place. Next, slipstitch all round the edges, on the wrong side.

Feather-stitching, with toning or brightly-contrasting embroidery silk or cotton is the favourite stitch for "crazy" (appliqué) patchwork, but I use it for the "piece" kind, too.

You may prefer chain stitch or back stitch, both equally effective.

"Crazy" patchwork, which is the easiest form of appliqué, has no planned design. Irregular shapes and sizes of material are stitched on to a foundation of very strong material, such as cotton sheeting or soft hessian.

You make up your design as you go along, using pieces of different sizes, but you should plan the colour mixing. Slipstitch each patch firmly in place and then outline with a fine chain stitch or featherstitch.

Here are some suggestions for making up your patchwork fabric into something beautiful, useful, and lasting: cushion covers, aprons, bags, table mats, chair seats (padded), quilts—as well as ideas which will occur to you, once you have started this fascinating hobby.

Patience you will need! But the satisfaction of seeing your work grow will increase as you add "just one more patch" before you put it aside for the day.